WALK ON WATER FAITH

CATHERINE MARTIN

WALK ON WATER FAITH

QuietTime
MINISTRIES
PALM DESERT, CALIFORNIA

Cover by Quiet Time Ministries.
Cover photo by Catherine Martin—myPhotoWalk.com

Interior photos by Catherine Martin available at MYPHOTOWALK.COM—CATHERINEMARTIN.SMUGMUG.COM

Walk On Water Fatih—Discovering Power In The Promises of God
Copyright © 2014 by Catherine Martin
Published by Quiet Time Ministries
Palm Desert, California 92255
www.quiettime.org

ISBN-13: 978-0-9905821-0-6

Printed in the United States of America
14 15 16 17 18 19 20 21 22 / ACS / 10 9 8 7 6 5 4 3 2 1

Dedicated to …
the One who is the author and perfecter of my faith,
the Lord Jesus Christ.

Dedicated to my husband
David G. Martin M.D.,
who has been my beloved companion
for thirty-two years
on this journey of faith.

Dedicated to
all those hearts who have taken God at His Word
in every generation.
Thank you for being my example
of how to run my race by faith
and live in God's promises.

May we become like the heroes
in God's Gallery of Faith in Hebrews 11,
those who have…
a walk on water faith.

For we walk by faith, not by sight.

2 CORINTHIANS 5:7

~

*And Peter got out of the boat, and walked on the water
and came toward Jesus.*

MATTHEW 14:29

~

*For whatever is born of God
overcomes the world;
and this is the victory
that has overcome the world—
our faith.*

1 JOHN 5:4

~

*And without faith
it is impossible to please Him,
for he who comes to God must believe that He is
and that He is a rewarder of those who seek Him.*

HEBREWS 11:6

CONTENTS

❧ INTRODUCTION ❧

It was the beginning of a new year. I wanted to spend some time with the Lord out in the beauty of His creation. So I grabbed my camera just before sunrise and headed to a nearby lake in hopes of taking photos of Canadian geese I had seen in the area. I arrived to find something quite unexpected and magnificent. Ten snowy white egrets were at the lake that day—an unusual occurrence! In the next hour, I experienced a glimpse of the spectacular glory of God. I saw things that perhaps only God sees sometimes. I watched mesmerized as these egrets flew back and forth across the water, playing with the surface by dancing on it, dragging their feet across the waves. One particularly heroic egret tried walking on the two wires that stretched across part of the water, one foot on each wire. And I noticed one thing in particular about all these egrets that day. They were not interested in swimming in the water. They wanted to walk, dance, and glide across the shimmering surface. They soared back and forth *walking on the water,* and yes, they even appeared to dance. Of course, I captured as many photos as I possibly could of this unique wonder. And I gave God a standing ovation.

That morning out in God's creation with those dancing egrets profoundly impacted me. I thought about our own need to dance on the surface of the waters of life, above the temporal things, instead of sinking below the water, crushed and defeated by the storm's fiercest elements. The last two years have been the most difficult of my life. Four people dearest to my heart went home to be with the Lord. One was my dear mentor and friend who served on the Board of Directors for Quiet Time Ministries. Another dear friend and mentor was a fellow author and encouraged me in the writing of my books. Another friend of mine who was well known in the entertainment world, and had written the song "Quiet Time" based on principles I teach in Quiet Time Ministries, also stepped into heaven. And then, this last year I walked through the long battle of cancer with my father, and I watched as he stepped into the presence of the Lord, now face to face with Him. I entered what I call the valley of the shadow. In that valley I have wrestled with discouragement and despair, brokenness and sadness.

In the middle of this valley, God took me to the lake and showed me the magnificent dance of the snowy white egrets. Had I not risen early, grabbed my camera, and driven to the water, I would have missed the whole thing. And how often do we just miss it? The Lord showed me that day there are wonders He has for me, eternal truths for me to learn, and majestic views of Him still unknown for me to experience. This was the beginning of something powerful God has been teaching me. Quiet time with Him is a priority and we must be intentional about it, setting aside a time, a place, and a plan to be alone with Him.

Then, the Lord took me to Romans 12:2 in the New Living Translation: "Don't copy the behavior and customs of this world, but let God transform you into a new person by changing the way you think. Then you will learn to know God's will for you, which is good and pleasing and perfect." These words powerfully pierced my heart. I began praying, "Lord, change the way I think. Then I will be transformed." Almost immediately, my quiet times deepened even further with the Lord as I applied something new. An idea came to my mind, "I'm going to ask God for a promise each day. It may come out of my Bible reading and study, a devotional, or a book in my quiet time." So every day I looked for one promise, and then wrote it in my journal. I carried it with me through the day. I lived in these promises. God used the promises from His Word to change the way I was thinking and to transform me. I experienced joy even in sorrow, hope in the midst of darkness, and peace in turbulent circumstances. How was this possible?

What God was teaching me in a new and deeper way was how to walk and live by faith in the most desperate times of life. I have been focused on learning about faith for many years. Because of my desire to be a faith-walking person, I have invested hours and hours in knowing and loving God and His Word. I love the Word of God. I carry it with me wherever I go. But now I was learning anew to live in God's Word, especially His promises. His promises are the secret to hope, one of the great results of a life of faith. In my book, *Walking with The God Who Cares*, I shared the definition of hope that the Lord gave me—*holding on with patient expectation*. In that book I wrote about the importance of finding the promise, embracing the promise, trusting the promise, and living the promise. But now, God took me deeper, and through living in His promises, I was growing in my faith and trust in Him.

This book is written that you may grow in your faith and discover the ability to walk on the water above and through every difficulty, and yes, even dance, just like those beautiful birds. Peter Kuzmic writes, "Hope is the ability to listen to the music of the future. Faith is the ability to dance to it in the present." The music is the Word of God, and when you hear it, you can dance, even through difficult circumstances in life.

Walk on Water Faith is going to take you into the lives of many characters in the Bible, men and women of God who learned how to walk by faith even when they were faced with challenging situations. The writer of Hebrews said it so well: "Remember those who led you, who spoke the word of God to you; and considering the result of their conduct, imitate their faith" (Hebrews 13:7). God has given us many examples of victorious heroes of faith, especially in Hebrews 11, God's Gallery of Faith, and often the best way to learn is by example. You will study Jesus' words about faith and watch how He taught His disciples many faith lessons. Each day of study includes one of my devotional photographs along with a promise from God to hold onto in your life. You will be encouraged to ask God for a promise a day from your quiet time to write on special A Promise A Day pages in the Appendix of this study. What a journey we are going to take together! My desire for you is that you won't just read about faith. No, I want you to actually live and walk by faith, and stand strong, unshaken by life's trials. Oh how the Lord loves it when we walk by faith! My desire is that we will all have a life that glorifies Him and brings a smile to the Lord's face, and that we will receive the very applause of heaven, hearing those amazing words, "Well done, good and faithful servant."

Together we will embark on this journey through Scripture in the form of quiet times alone with the Lord. Each quiet time is organized according to the PRAYER™ Quiet Time Plan™:

Prepare Your Heart

Read and Study God's Word

Adore God in Prayer

Yield Yourself to God

Enjoy His Presence

Rest in His Love

Each week consists of five days of quiet times, photo selections from my devotional photography, and then a devotional reading on Days 6-7. Each quiet time includes devotional reading, devotional

Bible study, journaling, prayer, worship, hymns, and application of God's Word. Journal Pages and Prayer Pages (adapted from *The Quiet Time Notebook*) to record your thoughts and prayers are in the Appendix of this book. A Promise A Day pages are also in the Appendix. With *Walk on Water Faith* and your Bible you have everything you need for rich quiet times with the Lord. Because schedules vary, you can be flexible and you may choose to take more than one day for each quiet time. You may complete each quiet time at your own pace, taking as little or as much time as you can give to spend alone with the Lord. If you desire to learn more about how to have a quiet time, I encourage you to get my book *Six Secrets to a Powerful Quiet Time*. To learn more about different kinds of devotional Bible studies for your quiet time, I encourage you to read my book *Knowing and Loving the Bible*.

VIEWER GUIDES

At the end of each week you will find your Viewer Guide to take notes from the video message. In each message, Catherine teaches from God's Word, and challenges you to draw near to the Lord. These inspirational and instructional messages are especially designed to accompany your studies each week. These messages are available on the companion *Walk on Water Faith* DVDs, downloadable Digital M4V Video, downloadable Digital MP3 Audio, as well as HD 1080p Digital M4V of the HD Leader's Kits for a professional large group experience. Search the Quiet Time Ministries Online Store at www.quiettime.org or call Quiet Time Ministries at 1-800-925-6458.

FOR LEADERS

Walk on Water Faith is a powerful resource for group study including a complete Leader's Guide with Discussion Questions in the Appendix. *Walk on Water Faith* DVD Leader's Kits or *Walk on Water Faith* HD 1080p Digital Leader's Kits are available at the Quiet Time Ministries Online Store at www.quiettime.org. You may also call Quiet Time Ministries at 1-800-925-6458. The kit includes the *Walk on Water Faith* book, *Walk on Water Faith* 9 video messages, *The Quiet Time Journal*, and the Quiet Time Ministries Signature Tote. Each *Walk on Water Faith* book is organized into 8 weeks with 5 days of quiet time per week and Days 6-7 for review and meditation. The book also includes 9 Viewer Guides for the group video sessions, Leader's Guide and Discussion Questions, and Journal and Prayer Pages.

QUIET TIME MINISTRIES ONLINE

Quiet Time Ministries Online at www.quiettime.org is a place where you can deepen your devotion to God and His Word. Cath's Blog is where Catherine shares about life, about the Lord, and just about everything else. A Walk In Grace™ is Catherine's devotional photojournal, highlighting her own myPhotoWalk photography, where you can grow deep in the garden of His grace. myQuietTime is an exclusive weekly HD 1080p video presented on YouTube at The Quiet Time Live Channel. myPhotoWalk.com is Catherine's devotional photography website where you can view her nature and landscape photography and order custom prints at CatherineMartin. SmugMug.com. You are also invited to join Catherine on Facebook, Twitter, and GooglePlus.

MY LETTER TO THE LORD

As you begin these quiet times, I'd like to ask, where are you? What has been happening in your life over the last year or so? What has been your life experience? What are you facing and what has God been teaching you? It is no accident that you are in this book of quiet times, *Walk on Water Faith*. In fact, God has something He wants you to know, something that will change the whole landscape of your experience with Him. Watch for it, listen for it, and when you learn it, write it down and never let it go. Will you write a prayer in the form of a letter to the Lord in the space provided expressing all that is on your heart and ask Him to speak to you in these quiet times?

My Letter To The Lord

Faith When The Wind Blows Hard

Welcome to *Walk On Water Faith*, a study on faith. In this study in God's Word, you are going to discover promises from God's Word that will strengthen your faith in the difficult circumstances of life. These Viewer Guides are designed to give you a place to write notes from my *Walk On Water Faith* messages available on DVDs, Digital M4V Video, and Digital MP3 Audio for your computer or mobile device. In our time together today, we are going to look at the words of Jesus and His encouragement to build your life in such a way that it will stand even in the storms of life.

"Therefore everyone who hears these words of Mine and acts on them, may be compared to a wise man who built his house on the rock" (Matthew 7:24).

How can we stand strong when the winds blow hard — Observations from Matthew 7:24-28

1. Your life is like a building project that is in the process of being _____.

Two kinds of buildings: On _____ or _____.

Be _____ and build on the rock.

2. How you handle the _____ of God determines the outcome of the building of your life.

Pay attention to the _____. Give high priority to God's Word in your life.

3. The _____ will come and slam against our life.

Be _____ for the storm. Don't be surprised.

4. Jesus wants us to build our life on the rock of His _____.

The definition of faith is taking God at His _____.

_____ on the Word.

What is going to help you in the building of a life on the rock of God's Word?

1. Get a _____ you love.

2. Have a Bible reading _____ to be in the Word every day.

3. Join a Bible _____ in a small group.

4. _____ a Bible with you wherever you go.

5. Take your Bible to _____ .

≈ *Video messages are available on DVDs or as Digital M4V Video. Audio messages are available as Digital MP3 Audio. Visit the Quiet Time Ministries Online Store at www.quiettime.org.*

FINDING FAITH WHEN THE WIND BLOWS HARD

Matthew 14:22-33

I believe in Christianity as I believe that the sun has risen: not only because I see it, but because by it I see everything else.

C.S. Lewis

THE WALK OF FAITH

And Peter got out of the boat, and walked on the water and came toward Jesus.

MATTHEW 14:29

PREPARE YOUR HEART

At the age of six weeks, Fanny Crosby lost her vision and was blind for the rest of her 94 years of life. At the age of eight, she wrote her first recorded lines of poetry: "O what a happy soul am I! Although I cannot see, I am resolved that in this world, contented I will be. How many blessings I enjoy, that other people don't. To weep and sigh because I'm blind, I cannot and I won't." Those are words from a young girl who walked with more sight than most people. They are words of someone who had learned how to walk by faith and, as a result, experienced great vision in life. Fanny Crosby became the beloved writer of more than eight thousand hymns, including Blessed Assurance, To God Be The Glory, and All The Way My Savior Leads Me.

How is your vision these days? Are you practiced at seeing the details of circumstances yet have no sight into God's hand at work in the midst of your life? C.S. Lewis says, "I believe in Christianity as I believe that the sun has risen: not only because I see it, but because by it I see everything else." When you walk by faith, you have true sight and real vision. Paul says that "we walk by faith, not by sight" (2 Corinthians 5:7). Does that mean we are actually blind as Christians or that we are to close our physical eyes? No. The exact opposite is true. You can finally see. Faith is real sight. But you see with the eyes of your heart, and your sight moves from the temporal to the eternal, into the realm those who don't walk by faith can never see. You see God—who He is, what He does, and what He says. When you are new in your faith, you may see only the bare outlines of God at work in your life. But as you grow in faith, the Lord becomes more clear to you. By faith, relying on God and His Word, you experience the ability to make it through difficult storms in life and stand strong, unshaken, even when the wind blows hard. And maybe you are in a trial where you are faced with the impossible. Be assured, dear friend, that nothing is too hard for God and He specializes in impossible situations.

Today, you are beginning a new study into a way and walk of life focusing on the eternal—the life of faith. In this faith walk, your vision will be stretched and you will be taken to mountaintops where you will see what others cannot even begin to fathom. Oh how great is this walk of faith where you will indeed walk on top of the turbulent waters of circumstantial events, gliding above and through great storms in life. And you will experience the great power and presence of Christ Himself. The life of faith is, as Corrie ten Boom wrote, a "fantastic adventure in trusting Him."

Don't you long to be strong in faith, and learn the secrets from God's Word that lead to spiritual maturity and great trust in God? In this first week of quiet times, you will study what faith is, why you need it, and how you can have the kind of faith that walks on water in difficult times of life.

Today, as you begin your study, draw near to the Lord in a quiet place and ask Him to speak to you in the deepest places of your soul. Write a prayer to Him, expressing all that is on your heart at the outset of these quiet times on faith.

READ AND STUDY GOD'S WORD

1. In 2 Corinthians 5:6-9, Paul is talking about our life on earth compared with life in heaven, face to face with the Lord. And he concludes by saying that our ambition while living on earth is "to be pleasing to Him (the Lord)." He explains the secret to having courage, knowing these eternal truths, and living to please the Lord. Read the great words of Paul in 2 Corinthians 5:7 describing how we are to live our life. Write this verse out, word for word.

2. Jesus is the Master Teacher and He has great lessons of faith for His disciples. One lesson occurred on a stormy night where the wind blew hard. Read about this event in Matthew 14:22-33. Describe what happened in 2-3 sentences.

3. The issue in this event is faith. Jesus told Peter that he had "little faith." What is faith? The Greek word for faith is *pistis* and means a firm persuasion, conviction, and belief in the truth. Ney

Bailey, author of *Faith is Not a Feeling*, defines it this way: "Faith is taking God at His Word."[1] And how are we able to "take God at His Word" when we are faced with severe storms in our lives? Walk on water faith is the ability to see beyond temporal circumstances to the eternal realities of God and His promises, and as a result, take God at His Word and act on His promises in spite of conflicting circumstances, thoughts, and feelings. Considering these definitions of faith, when do you think Peter demonstrated faith and what do you think encouraged his faith?

ADORE GOD IN PRAYER

Use the words of this prayer from *The Valley of Vision* as a prayer of faith today:

MY GOD,

I bless thee that thou hast given me the eye of faith,

to see thee as Father,

to know thee as a covenant God,

to experience thy love planted in me;

For faith is the grace of union

by which I spell out my entitlement to thee;

Faith casts my anchor upwards where I trust in thee

and engage thee to be my Lord.

Be pleased to live and move within me,

breathing in my prayers,

inhabiting my praises,

speaking in my words,

moving in my actions,

living in my life,

causing me to grow in grace.

Thy bounteous goodness has helped me believe,

but my faith is weak and wavering,

its light dim,

its steps tottering,

its increase slow,

its backslidings frequent;

It should scale the heavens but lies grovelling in the dust.
Lord, fan this divine spark into glowing flame.
When faith sleeps, my heart becomes an unclean thing,
the fount of every loathsome desire, the cage of unclean lusts
all fluttering to escape, the noxious tree of deadly fruit,
the open wayside of earthly tares.
Lord, awake faith to put forth its strength
until all heaven fills my soul and all impurity is cast out.[2]

THE VALLEY OF VISION

YIELD YOURSELF TO GOD

Faith is that God-given ability that, when exercised, brings the unseen into plain view. It deals with the supernatural and makes impossible things possible. And yes, it grows during storms—that is, it grows through disturbances in the spiritual atmosphere…it is in this atmosphere of conflict that faith finds its most fertile soil and grows most rapidly to maturity. The strongest trees are found not in the thick shelter of the forest but out in the open, where winds from every direction bear down upon them. The fierce winds bend and twist them until they become giant in stature…The path of faith is one of sorrow and joy, suffering and healing comfort, tears and smiles, trials and victories, conflicts and triumphs, and also hardships, dangers, beatings, persecutions, misunderstanding, trouble, and distress. Yet "in all these things we are more than conquerors through Him who loved us" (Romans 8:37).

E.A. KILBOURNE IN STREAMS IN THE DESERT

When the winds begin to rise, and a storm threatens—it is time to get our spiritual tackling ready and to cast anchor. The mariner casts his anchor downward; the Christian casts his anchor upward within the veil. In the deepest danger, he casts out the sweet anchor of faith and is not afraid. So says the text, "He shall not be afraid of evil tidings; his heart is fixed, trusting in the Lord" (Psalm 112:7)…

THOMAS WATSON

The children of God are on their way to the Father's house. As spiritual voyagers they are homeward-bound. Heaven is the place at which they will as certainly arrive as Christ Himself is there. Already the expectant of glory binds the "wave sheaf" to his believing bosom. Faith is the spiritual spy of the soul. It travels far into the promised land, gathers the ripe clusters—the evidences and pledges of its reality and richness—and, returning, bears with it these, the "first-fruits" of the coming vintage.[3]

Octavius Winslow in Help Heavenward

Enjoy His Presence

Where are you in your faith right now? Are you taking God at His Word? If faith is "the spiritual spy of the soul" as Octavius Winslow writes, are you opening God's Word to gaze long into the eternal things of the Lord? As you read about Peter and his walk on the water, what part of his experience can you identify with the most—fear in the night storm, a call to Jesus in prayer, getting out of the boat, walking on water above the storm, or sinking into the tumultuous waves? Write out your thoughts, then read the words of Paul in 2 Corinthians 5:7 again. Memorize those words and take them with you throughout the day. Then, ask God for a promise from your quiet time today and write it in A Promise A Day in the Appendix of this book. Close by looking at the photo and promise on the next page, then write a prayer, asking the Lord to grow you into a person who walks by faith, not by sight.

REST IN HIS LOVE

"For we walk by faith, not by sight" (2 Corinthians 5:7).

SPRINGS IN THE VALLEYS

I will open rivers on the bare heights and springs in the midst of the valleys. Isaiah 41:18
Zion National Park, Utah, USA
Nikon D7000, ISO 125, f14.0, 1/200, Adobe Photoshop, Nik Silver Efex Pro
MYPHOTOWALK.COM—CATHERINEMARTIN.SMUGMUG.COM

FAITH WHEN YOU NEED IT MOST

But the boat was already a long distance from the land, battered by the waves; for the wind was contrary. And in the fourth watch of the night He came to them, walking on the sea.

MATTHEW 14:24-25

PREPARE YOUR HEART

In March of 1849 the cholera epidemic sweeping across Europe reached New York. Fanny Crosby describes the time when the disease spread to the school where she taught. "We knew that the disease might enter our school at any moment: in which case we feared a terrible mortality among the pupils, for none of them had left for the summer vacation. On the following Monday we had our first case. One of the youngest girls was taken; she called me to her and asked me to hold her in my lap, as I had been accustomed to do...I shudder when I recall those days."[4] Not only did Fanny watch others suffer, but then she began experiencing symptoms of cholera herself. She knew she was facing possible death if she did, in fact, have the disease. For three days and nights, after taking medicine for cholera, she awoke after a good night's rest to find herself in perfect health. Following that time, she was sent out of the city until the danger passed. This time of trial served to challenge and ultimately, strengthen her faith.

Have you ever experienced a time when you are overcome with trouble in your life? The wind is blowing hard. The storm is raging. And you are feeling overwhelmed and afraid. You know how it is. It's nighttime, you're lying in bed, and all you can think about are your troubles. That's how it was for the disciples that night in the boat on the water. The fourth watch of the night was sometime between three and six in the morning. The disciples were caught in a storm and they didn't know if they would make it.

The fourth watch of the night is the time when you need faith the most. You need to hear from God and take Him at His Word. Perhaps you are experiencing the fourth watch even now. You will learn from the example of Peter that to have faith in the fourth watch you need to *look to Jesus* and *listen to Jesus*. Write a prayer to the Lord, asking Him to speak to you especially in the times when you need faith the most.

READ AND STUDY GOD'S WORD

1. Read Matthew 14:24-27 and describe what happened.

2. Remember the definition of faith we thought about yesterday? The short definition is: *Faith is taking God at His Word.* A longer definition that helps us understand walk on water faith is: *Faith is the ability to see beyond temporal circumstances to the eternal realities of God and His promises, and as a result, take God at His Word and act on His promises in spite of conflicting circumstances, thoughts, and feelings.* Underline "take God at His Word" and "act on His promises" in those definitions. Now, describe what Jesus did to encourage the disciples to exercise faith during the fourth watch of the night.

3. In the fourth watch of the night, Jesus came to His disciples. And He spoke to them. In the fourth watch of the night, to have faith, it is imperative that we look past the circumstances and *look to Jesus*, Who is with us, and *listen to Jesus*, Who is speaking to us in the Bible, His Word. When He spoke to those disciples, He gave them a great promise about Himself. Oh there is such power in the promises of God! They tell us Who He is, What He does, and What He says. The promises of God give us a solid foundation and never change. We can stand strong, unshaken and courageous, in the face of any storm with God's promises in His Word.

Jesus said, "Take courage, it is I; do not be afraid" (Matthew 14:27). The Greek for "it is I" is *ego eimi*, the same name revealed by God to Moses: "I AM" (Exodus 3:14). In the name, I AM, God reveals that He is Yahweh, the One who is everything you need for every circumstance of life. In the gospel of John, Jesus revealed Himself to be Yahweh (I AM—*ego eimi*) often. One of the most exciting times was in a conversation with those who were challenging His identity. He replied in John 8:58, "Truly, truly I say to you, before Abraham was born, I am." The people picked up stones to throw at Him, recognizing His claim to be God. With this in mind, what did Jesus want His disciples to realize out there on the water, in the wind, and during the fourth watch of the night when He said as He was walking on the water, "Take courage, it is I; do not be afraid"?

4. Included in the longer definition of faith is the fact that you will see beyond the temporal to the eternal. This eternal perspective is "the ability to see all of life from God's point of view and have what you see affect how you live in the present."[5] The eternal perspective is really the ability to walk and live by faith. Read the words of Paul in 2 Corinthians 4:16-18. How do these words help you in understanding how to have faith?

5. The Lord is speaking in His Word and desires us to listen to Him in every circumstance of life. Read the following verses and record what you learn about God's Word:

Psalm 119:105

Isaiah 40:8

John 17:17

Romans 10:17, 15:4

2 Timothy 3:16-17

Hebrews 4:12

2 Peter 1:4

6. Considering these verses, why is God's Word essential and why are His promises so encouraging in the fourth watches of the night?

7. God's Word is filled with commands and promises to encourage your faith in fourth watches of the night. These commands and promises show you who God is and what He does. In every circumstance, faith involves the ability to look to your Lord—*look to Jesus* and *listen to Jesus* as He speaks in His Word. Read the following promises and underline your favorite words and phrases for encouragement in a fourth watch of the night:

> "The righteous cry, and the LORD hears and delivers them out of all their troubles. The LORD is near to the brokenhearted and saves those who are crushed in spirit" (Psalm 34:17-18).

> "My soul, wait in silence for God only, for my hope is from Him. He only is my rock and my salvation, my stronghold; I shall not be shaken. On God my salvation and my glory rest; the rock of my strength, my refuge is in God. Trust in Him at all times, O people; pour out your heart before Him; God is a refuge for us" (Psalm 62:5-8).

> "When I remember You on my bed, I meditate on You in the night watches, for You have been my help, and in the shadow of Your wings I sing for joy. My soul clings to You; Your right hand upholds me" (Psalm 63:6-8).

> "For a day in Your courts is better than a thousand outside. I would rather stand at the threshold of the house of my God than dwell in the tents of wickedness. For the LORD God is a sun and shield; The LORD gives grace and glory; No good thing does He withhold from those who walk uprightly. O LORD of hosts, how blessed is the man who trusts in You!" (Psalm 84:10-12).

"Do not fear, for I am with you; do not anxiously look about you, for I am your God. I will strengthen you, surely I will help you, surely I will uphold you with My righteous right hand" (Isaiah 41:10).

ADORE GOD IN PRAYER

Pray the following prayer by Corrie ten Boom:
Open our eyes, dear Lord, that we may see the far vast reaches of eternity,
Help us to look beyond life's little cares so prone to fret us
And the grief that wears our courage thin.
O may we tune our hearts to Thy great harmony
That all the parts may ever be in perfect, sweet accord.
Give us Thine own clear vision, blessed Lord.[6]

YIELD YOURSELF TO GOD

True faith must be based solely on scriptural facts, for "faith cometh by hearing, and hearing by the word of God" (Romans 10:17). Unless our faith is established on facts, it is no more than conjecture, superstition, speculation or presumption.[7]

MILES STANFORD IN PRINCIPLES OF SPIRITUAL GROWTH

Faith is dependence upon God. And this God-dependence only begins when self-dependence ends. And self-dependence only comes to its end, with some of us, when sorrow, suffering, affliction, broken plans and hopes brings us to that place of self-helplessness and defeat. And only then do we find that we have learned the lesson of faith; to find our tiny craft of life rushing onward to a blessed victory of life and power and service undreamt of in the days of fleshly strength and self-reliance.

JAMES MCCONKEY

ENJOY HIS PRESENCE

How is God encouraging you to take Him at His Word? What promise is significant today in your study (write it in A Promise A Day). Have you learned the value of His Word for your fourth watch of the night? Do you realize that the Bible is not just words on a page. It is the Word of God.

How is He helping you look past the temporal circumstances to His promises about Himself and what He will do in your life? Take a few moments to drink in the beauty of your Lord's majestic creation in the devotional photography on this page. Then, write a prayer to the Lord as you talk with Him about all you've learned. You may wish to write out your prayer requests on a Prayer page in the back of this book. Watch expectantly to see how the Lord answers your prayers.

REST IN HIS LOVE

"Your word is a lamp to my feet and a light to my path" (Psalm 119:105).

THE LORD MY ROCK

The LORD is my rock and my fortress and my deliverer. Psalm 18:2
Zion National Park, Utah, USA
Nikon D7000, ISO 160, f11.0, 0.4, Adobe Photoshop, Nik Silver Efex Pro
MYPHOTOWALK.COM—CATHERINEMARTIN.SMUGMUG.COM

THE SAY-SO OF THE LORD

But immediately Jesus spoke to them, saying, "Take courage, it is I; do not be afraid."
MATTHEW 14:27

PREPARE YOUR HEART

Do you remember, as a child, hearing your parents or someone in authority telling you something you needed to know, do, or obey? And more than once, you may have asked, "Why do I have to do this?" Or, "Why do I need to know this?" And the reply was, "Because I said so."

When God speaks, He is giving you His "say-so", and He is expecting your ready response. To have faith in the fourth watch of the night, not only do *we look to Jesus* and *listen to Jesus*, but then we *respond to Jesus*.

The Lord can be trusted and all He says is true. It is impossible for Him to lie and He stands behind everything He says (Hebrews 6:18). When He gives you a promise, He desires your belief, reliance, and trust in all that He says. You are then responding by faith, taking Him at His Word. For example, if He says He loves you, that's His say-so with the expectation of your belief that you are, in fact, loved by God. Even if you don't feel loved, you know you are, because God has said so. With every statement, command, or promise from God, there is a corresponding say-so on your part, filled with resolve to live by what He has said to you.

The perfect example of God's say-so and man's corresponding say-so, resolve, and responses is found in Hebrews 13:5-6. "He Himself has said, 'I will never desert you, nor will I ever forsake you,' so that we confidently say, 'The LORD is my helper, I will not be afraid. What will man do to me?'" Knowing that God has promised to never leave us moves us to say He will help us and now, there is no need to fear. This principle of response to God's Word is so important for us to know in our understanding of faith. David, in his psalms, is a perfect example of God's say-so and the corresponding words, resolve, and actions of faith from David. "When You said, 'Seek My face,' my heart said to You, 'Your face, O LORD, I shall seek'" (Psalm 27:8). Another example is seen in Psalm 28:7 when David discovers "the LORD is my strength and my shield." He responds by saying, "My heart trusts in Him, and I am helped; therefore my heart exults, and with my song I shall thank Him."

God speaks, and His words imply new actions and beliefs on our part. Through His Word, in the power of His Spirit, we are changed. We grow deeper in our faith and become more than we are right now. We are transformed. God desires to make you a faith-walking person. And "He is at work in you, both to will and to work for His good pleasure (Philippians 2:13). Ask Him now to speak to you as you draw near to Him today.

READ AND STUDY GOD'S WORD

1. Read Matthew 14:24-27 again. Describe how the disciples were feeling in the storm they were experiencing.

2. Imagine that you are in the boat with those disciples on the Sea of Galilee. And now you look out across the stormy sea, and you see a Person walking out there on the waves of the water. The disciples in the boat cried out in fear with the thought they were seeing a ghost! Jesus immediately spoke an amazing promise to them, "Take courage, it is I; do not be afraid" (Matthew 14:27). In those words, we realize that Jesus wanted those disciples and us to know that it was not a ghost on the water, but instead, Yahweh, the One who is everything we need for every circumstance of life. Because He was with them, taking an enjoyable stroll on top of the waves He Himself had created, He wanted them to be courageous instead of terrified, worried, and anxious. Oh just think of the power of that promise wrapped up in the name of God revealed by Jesus in the fourth watch of the night. No wonder He was assuring them not to be terrified, and instead to take courage. The word "courage" in this context means to be bold, cheerful, comforted, and confident.

When Jesus speaks, He expects a response. To have faith in the fourth watch of the night we need to *respond to Jesus*. Now read Matthew 14:28-29 and describe what Peter said in response to Jesus' words, what Jesus said, and what Peter did as a result.

3. What was necessary on Peter's part in response to the words of Jesus, "Come" (Matthew 14:29)?

4. Oh yes, Peter got out of the boat and walked on the water. Despite the fourth watch of the night, the pouring rain, and the wild wind, Peter was walking on top of the waves and through the storm. And the same is possible for you, when you live by faith, taking God at His Word. You are able to make it through the most difficult circumstances in life. Walking on water with your faith means you defy the defeat of the circumstance and literally make it through to the other side. You are enabled and empowered by the very presence and power of Jesus in the midst of your adversity or challenge. You experience real triumph and victory. Read the following verses and write what you learn about difficulties, the life of faith, and the Lord's desire for us.

John 16:33

1 John 5:4-5

5. Finally, read these words from Number 23:19 and underline your favorite truths about God and His Word. As you read this amazing promise from God, think about why there is such power in His promises. "God is not a man, that He should lie, nor a son of man, that He should repent; Has He said, and will He not do it? Or Has He spoken, and will He not make it good?"

ADORE GOD IN PRAYER

O my refuge, outside You the waves are high and the winds fierce, but in You I have haven, protection, peace, and blessedness. You are my pavilion, my refuge, my strong tower, the house of my defense, my shield and exceeding great reward. In You I make my refuge.[8]

F.B. MEYER IN DAILY PRAYERS

YIELD YOURSELF TO GOD

What line does my thought take? Does it turn to what God says or to what I fear…as we go on in grace we find that God is glorifying Himself here and now, in the present minute. If we have God's say-so behind us, the most amazing strength comes, and we learn to sing in the ordinary days and ways…My say-so is to be built on God's say-so…I will not be haunted by apprehension. This does not mean that I will not be tempted to fear, but I will remember God's say-so…Get hold of the Father's say-so, and then say with good courage—"I will not fear."[9]

OSWALD CHAMBERS IN MY UTMOST FOR HIS HIGHEST

When the Lord calls you to come across the water, step out with confidence and joy. And never glance away from Him for even a moment. You will not prevail by measuring the waves or grow strong by gauging the wind…Lift up your eyes to the hills (Psalm 121:1) and go forward. There is no other way. *Do you fear to launch away? Faith lets go to swim! Never will He let you go; It's by trusting you will know fellowship with Him.*

STREAMS IN THE DESERT

That is genuine faith—believing and declaring what God has said, stepping out on what appears to be thin air and finding solid rock beneath your feet. Therefore boldly declare what God says you have…The moment has come when you must jump from your perch of distrust, leaving the nest of supposed safety behind and trusting the wings of faith. You must be like a young bird beginning to test the air with its untried wings…we know the air is there and that the air is not nearly as insubstantial as it seems. And you know that the promises of God are there, and they certainly are not insubstantial at all…If God has said so, surely you do not want to suggest He has lied! If He has spoken, will He not fulfill it? If He has given you His word—His sure word of promise—do not question it but trust it absolutely. You have His promise, and in fact you have even more—you have Him who confidently speaks the words.

STREAMS IN THE DESERT

Our Lord is constantly taking us into the dark, that He may tell us things. Into the dark of the shadowed home, where bereavement has drawn the blinds; into the dark of the lonely, desolate life, where some infirmity closes us in from the light and stir of life; into the dark of some crushing sorrow and disappointment. Then He tells us His secrets, great and wonderful, eternal and infinite; He causes the eye which has become dazzled by the glare of earth to behold the heavenly constellations; and the ear to detect the undertones of His voice, which is often drowned amid the tumult of earth's strident cries. But such revelations always imply a corresponding responsibility—"that speak ye in the light—that proclaim upon the housetops." We are not meant to always linger in the dark, or stay in the closet; presently we shall be summoned to take our place in the rush and storm of life; and when that moment comes, we are to speak and proclaim what we have learned…God has a purpose in it all. He has withdrawn His child to the higher altitudes of fellowship, that he may hear God speaking face to face, and bear the message to his fellows at the mountain foot…there is no short cut to the life of faith, which is the all-vital condition of a holy and victorious life. We must have periods of lonely meditation and fellowship with God. That our souls should have their mountains of fellowship, their valley of quiet rest beneath the shadow of a great rock, their nights beneath the stars, when darkness has veiled the material and silenced the stir of human life, and has opened the view of the infinite and eternal, is as indispensable as that our bodies should have food.

F.B. Meyer in Streams in the Desert

Hope is the ability to listen to the music of the future. Faith is the courage to dance to it in the present.

Dr. Peter Kuzmic

Enjoy His Presence

Dear friend, have you heard the Word of the Lord today? Now, what will you say in response? What will you resolve for your own life in light of God's "say-so," His promise to you, so that you can experience the victory of faith? Will you be the one to have a walk on water faith? How do you need to get out of the boat in your own life? Write out your thoughts and insights in your Journal. Write your favorite promise from God's Word in A Promise A Day, then carry it with you throughout the day. Take a few moments to drink in the beauty of your Lord's handiwork in the devotional photography on this page, remembering He can paint beauty into the landscape of your life.

REST IN HIS LOVE

"For whatever is born of God overcomes the world; and this is the victory that has overcome the world—our faith. Who is the one who overcomes the world, but he who believes that Jesus is the Son of God" (1 John 5:4-5).

THE LORD WILL GUIDE YOU

The LORD will guide you continually, giving you water when you are dry. Isaiah 58:11
Zion National Park, Utah, USA
Nikon D7000, ISO 160, f11.0, 0.3, Adobe Photoshop, Nik Silver Efex Pro
MYPHOTOWALK.COM—CATHERINEMARTIN.SMUGMUG.COM

WHEN YOUR FAITH IS CHALLENGED

But seeing the wind, he became frightened, and beginning to sink, he cried out, "Lord, save me!" Immediately Jesus stretched out His hand and took hold of him, and said to him, "You of little faith, why did you doubt?"

MATTHEW 14:30-31

PREPARE YOUR HEART

What do you look at in life? The wind or the Word of God? That's really what it comes down to when you are journeying through the circumstances of life. The wind may blow or it may be calm. We are tempted either way to take our eyes away from God and the promises in His Word and look intently at the circumstances and focus on the temporal. Instead, our gaze must turn to the eternal truth found in God's Word. In His Word we realize the greatness and glory of God, and the opportunity to experience His power and presence in our lives. Paul writes, "For momentary, light affliction is producing for us an eternal weight of glory far beyond all comparison, while we look not at the things which are seen, but at the things which are not seen; for the things which are seen are temporal, but the things which are not seen are eternal" (2 Corinthians 4:17-18). In this one promise, we learn that trials are actually productive yielding a positive eternal result in the life of anyone who knows Christ.

Fanny Crosby, blind since the age of six months, experienced a momentary storm, when a well-meaning pastor remarked to her, "I think it is a great pity that the Master did not give you sight when He showered so many other gifts upon you." She replied quickly, "Do you know that if at birth I had been able to make one petition, it would have been that I should be born blind?" "Why?" asked the surprised minister. "Because when I get to heaven, the first face that shall ever gladden my sight will be that of my Savior!" Fanny Crosby could have chosen to turn her eyes from the truth of God and His Word, and sink under the wind of a thought that was not true. And though the words from the person may have stung momentarily, they were viewed in light of what Fanny knew in the Bible. And the same must be true for you. When your faith is challenged with contrary winds, you can know that your faith is being tested. Believe Jesus, be encouraged by a promise from the Lord, and keep your eyes fixed on Him and His Word.

Begin your time with the Lord today meditating on the words Fanny Crosby wrote as a prayer to the Lord:

> Hold Thou my hand; so weak I am, and helpless,
> I dare not take one step without Thy aid;
> Hold Thou my hand; for then, O loving Savior,
> No dread of ill shall make my soul afraid.
>
> Hold Thou my hand, and closer, closer draw me
> To Thy dear self—my hope, my joy, my all;
> Hold Thou my hand, lest haply I should wander,
> And, missing Thee, my trembling feet should fall.
>
> Hold Thou my hand; the way is dark before me
> Without the sunlight of Thy face divine;
> But when by faith I catch its radiant glory,
> What heights of joy, what rapturous songs are mine!
>
> Hold Thou my hand, that when I reach the margin
> Of that lone river Thou didst cross for me,
> A heavenly light may flash along its waters,
> And every wave like crystal bright shall be.

FANNY CROSBY, 1879

READ AND STUDY GOD'S WORD

1. Peter is such a great example for us when it comes to learning all about faith. When Peter realized the Lord Himself was out there walking on the water, he expressed boldness in his faith by asking the Lord to bring him out on the water. He had *looked to Jesus* and *listened to Jesus*. And now he was ready to *respond to Jesus*. Jesus said, "Come!" That was a promise from Jesus. He was

saying indeed Peter could walk on the water. And Peter responded and got out of the boat and walked on the water in the midst of the storm. How many of us actually dare to dream such majestic feats of faith as Peter did that early morning in the stormy waters? For Peter to walk on water with his faith, and respond to Jesus' promise, his faith involved getting out of the boat. In what ways do we need to "get out of the boat" to respond in faith to what God says?

2. Read Matthew 14:28-32 and write out what then happened to Peter once he got out there on the water. How was his faith being tested?

3. In light of Peter's response to the wind in Matthew 14:30, where do you think his attention, thoughts, and mind were focused once he saw the wind? And how much attention do you think Peter was giving the promise of Jesus at that moment when he saw the wind?

4. As you think about Jesus' words in Matthew 14:31 and Peter's response to the wind, what place do you think Jesus believes fear and doubt should have in our lives?

5. What kind of faith does Jesus want us to have? Once we have responded in faith, we need to continue to *believe Jesus*. How can we continue to believe Jesus when the wind continues to come our way in trials?

6. What did Peter do once he realized he was sinking and how did Jesus respond (see Matthew 14:30-31). How was Peter's action a demonstration of faith?

7. Look at the following verses about fear and underline those words and phrases that are most significant to you.

"The LORD is the one who goes ahead of you; He will be with you. He will not fail you or forsake you. Do not fear or be dismayed" (Deuteronomy 31:8)

"I sought the LORD, and He answered me, and delivered me from all my fears. They looked to Him and were radiant, and their faces will never be ashamed. This poor man cried, and the LORD heard him and saved him out of all his troubles" (Psalm 34:4-6).

"Don't be afraid, for I am with you. Don't be discouraged, for I am your God. I will strengthen you and help you. I will hold you up with my victorious right hand" (Isaiah 41:10 NLT).

ADORE GOD IN PRAYER

Pray the prayer of Peter Marshall today: "Forgive us, O God, for our small concept of the heart of the Eternal, for the doubting suspicion with which we regard the heart of God. Give to us more faith. We have so little…we say. Yet we have faith in each other—in checks and banks, in trains and airplanes, in cooks, and in strangers who drive us in cabs. Forgive us for our stupidity, that we have faith in people whom we do not know, and are so reluctant to have faith in Thee who knowest us altogether. We are always striving to find a complicated way through life when Thou hast a plan, and we refuse to walk in it. So many of our troubles we bring on ourselves. How silly we are…Wilt Thou give to us that faith that we can deposit in the bank of Thy love, so that we may receive the dividends and interest that Thou art so willing to give us. We ask it all in the lovely name of Jesus Christ our Saviour. Amen."[10]

YIELD YOURSELF TO GOD

We must be willing to live by faith, not hoping or desiring to live any other way. We must be willing to have every light around us extinguished, to have every star in the heaven blotted out, and to live with nothing encircling us but darkness and danger. Yes, we must be willing to do all this, if God will only leave within our soul an inner radiance from the pure, bright light that faith has kindled.

THOMAS C. UPHAM IN STREAMS IN THE DESERT

Where do you live? Some are living in doubt. Adverse circumstances, failure, and uncertainty have weakened faith; and the result is doubt. If you are numbered in the army of the doubters, you question the power of God—His power to save to the end, His power to guide through the perilous journey of life, His power to supply your needs. Possibly you doubt His promises, or the authenticity of His Word, the Bible…Rest on His unerring grace, and stand upon His promises. "Standing on the promises which cannot fail, when the howling storms of doubt and fear assail; by the living Word of God I shall prevail, standing on the promises of God." Are you living in doubt? You need not. Rest upon the infallible Word of God, which abides forever. Heaven and earth shall pass away, but He remains, ever the same, and His promises are yea and amen. Where do you live?[11]

ROBERT PARSONS IN QUOTES FROM THE QUIET HOUR

What did Jesus mean when He spoke of Peter as having "little faith"? D. Martyn Lloyd Jones, in his book, *Studies in the Sermon On The Mount*, helps us better understand these words in the context of anxiety and worry addressed by Jesus in His Sermon on the Mount. He writes: "To be of 'little faith' means, first of all, that we are mastered by our circumstances instead of mastering them…" Jones continues by writing about the anxieties the crowd listening to Jesus may have been thinking about: "There they are, as it were, sitting helplessly under a great cloud of concern about food and drink and clothing and many other things. These things are bearing down upon them, and they are the victims of them…" As we think about Peter's discouragement with the wind as he was walking on the water, D. Martyn Lloyd Jones helps us see the real truth that leads us to a "little faith." He writes: "Why does the man of little faith allow things to master him and to get him down? The answer to that question is that, in a sense, the real trouble with "little faith" is that it does not think…the whole trouble with a man of little faith is that he does not think. He allows circumstances to bludgeon him. That is the real difficulty in life. Life comes to us with a club in its hand and strikes us upon the head, and we become incapable of thought, helpless and defeated.

The way to avoid that, according to our Lord, is to think. We must spend more time in studying our Lord's lessons in observation and deduction. The Bible is full of logic, and we must never think of faith as something purely mystical. We do not just sit down in an armchair and expect marvellous things to happen to us. That is not the Christian faith. Christian faith is essentially thinking…The trouble with most people however, is that they will not think. Instead of doing this, they sit down and ask, What is going to happen to me? What can I do?…" The real secret, according to Jones is the importance of us thinking rightly in the context of adverse circumstances. He continues, "Faith, if you like, can be defined like this: It is a man insisting upon thinking when everything seems determined to bludgeon and knock him down in an intellectual sense. The trouble with the person of little faith is that, instead of controlling his own thought, his thought is being controlled by something else, and as we put it, he goes round and round in circles. That is the essence of worry…" And then, we see the importance of the Word of God for our faith: "Little faith, if you like, can also be described as a failure to take scriptural statements at their face value and to believe them utterly…This "little faith," is ultimately due to a failure to apply what we know, and claim to believe, to the circumstances and details of life…" Jones continues his encouragement to faith without worry by writing, "There is no circumstance or condition in this life which should lead a Christian to worry." He concludes with an encouragement to walk by faith: "Exercise faith; understand the truth and apply it to every detail of your life."[12]

ENJOY HIS PRESENCE

How is your faith being challenged right now? How do you need to get out of the boat? Are you focusing intently and responding to the wind or are you moving past the wind to give your attention and thoughts to everything God promises in His Word related to your situation? Have you learned to pray to Jesus like Peter did when you find yourself wavering in life? Do you live in fear and doubt or by faith in God's Word? What promise can you embrace, believe, and live in today? Write it out in A Promise A Day. Reflect on God's handiwork in the devotional image on the next page. Write your thoughts, then close with a prayer to the Lord.

REST IN HIS LOVE

"I sought the LORD, and He answered me, and delivered me from all my fears. They looked to Him and were radiant, and their faces will never be ashamed. This poor man cried, and the LORD heard him and saved him out of all his troubles" (Psalm 34:4-6).

THE TREES OF THE FIELD

And all the trees of the field will clap their hands. Isaiah 55:12
Zion National Park, Utah, USA
Nikon D7000, ISO 125, f11.0, 1/200, Adobe Photoshop, Nik Silver Efex Pro
MYPHOTOWALK.COM—CATHERINEMARTIN.SMUGMUG.COM

THE OBJECT OF YOUR FAITH

*When they got in the boat, the wind stopped. And those who were in
the boat worshiped Him, saying "You are certainly God's Son!"*

MATTHEW 14:32-33

PREPARE YOUR HEART

A radio talk show host once remarked, "My problem is that I have no faith." Many people throughout the world feel as though they are completely lacking in faith. And perhaps you have felt the same many times.

Every day we have confidence in something. We get in the car, put the key in the ignition, with faith that the car will start. We call people with our phones, believing that the phone will function as it is designed. We sit in a chair believing it will hold us steady and give us a place to rest.

Biblical faith is a gift of God. God has given us a measure of faith, according to Romans 12:3. And it is not humanly manufactured but God-given and God-enabled through the power of His Spirit (Galatians 2:20, 5:22). Faith is objective, resting on God and His Word. In the case of Peter, he looked away from the Lord and focused on the wind. At that moment, Peter had more confidence and trust in the wind than faith in the Word of the Lord and began to sink under the contrary wind and waves of the storm. The object of our faith must rightly be Jesus and all that He says. To have faith in the fourth watch, we need to *look to Jesus, listen to Jesus, respond to Jesus, believe Jesus, pray to Jesus,* and *worship Jesus.*

Today, the goal of your quiet time is to look at Peter's relationship with the Lord and all he learned about the Lord. Ask the Lord now to speak to you as you draw near to Him.

READ AND STUDY GOD'S WORD

1. Read Matthew 14:30-33 and describe what happened and how Peter got back to the boat.

2. What did the disciples learn about Jesus, what impressed them, and how did they express their faith?

47

3. In Matthew 14:31 Jesus said "You of little faith, why did you doubt?" Read Matthew 17:20-21 where Jesus contrasts "little faith" with "faith as small as a mustard seed." Write your own insight about mustard seed faith. In Jesus's words, we see the importance of the object of our faith. It's not how much faith but Who and what you put your faith in — quality of faith is more important than quantity. Mustard seed faith in a great God can move mountains of impossibilities.

4. In every situation, the Lord will show you something about Himself—Who He is, What He does, and What He says. And when you know Him more, you will trust Him, love Him and worship Him in a deeper way. Read the following verses and record what Peter learned about Jesus and how he grew in his relationship with Jesus, the object of his faith:

Mark 8:27-29

Luke 22:31-34 (Peter was also named Simon)

John 21:15-17

Optional: John 6:69, Acts 3:6-7, 4:8-14

ADORE GOD IN PRAYER

Pray the following prayer from Corrie ten Boom: "The human side in us fears the unknown, Lord. Give us the faith we need to step out of our dim caves and into Your guiding light."[13]

YIELD YOURSELF TO GOD

Standing on the promises of Christ my King,

Through eternal ages let His praises ring!

Glory in the highest I will shout and sing

Standing on the promises of God.

Refrain: Standing, standing,

Standing on the promises of God my Savior.

Standing, standing, I'm standing on the promises of God.

Standing on the promises that cannot fail

When the howling storms of doubt and fear assail;

By the living Word of God I shall prevail

Standing on the promises of God. *Refrain*

Standing on the promises of Christ the Lord,

Bound to Him eternally by love's strong cord,

Overcoming daily with the Spirit's sword

Standing on the promises of God. *Refrain*

Standing on the promises I cannot fall,

Listening every moment to the Spirit's call,

Resting in my Savior as my all in all

Standing on the promises of God. *Refrain*

R. Kelso Carter

Enjoy His Presence

Think about all you have learned from Peter this week about faith. What are the most important truths you've learned for your own walk of faith? Where in your life do you need to grow the most in order to have faith in the fourth watch when the wind is blowing hard in your life as you learn to look to Jesus, listen to Jesus, respond to Jesus, believe Jesus, pray to Jesus, and worship Jesus? What's your favorite promise today? Write it out in A Promise A Day. Write a prayer in your Journal, expressing all that is on your heart. Ask the Lord to help you, moment by moment, to walk by faith not by sight. Close by meditating on the beauty of God's creation seen in the devotional photography on the next page.

REST IN HIS LOVE

"And He continued by questioning them, 'But who do you say that I am?' Peter answered and said to Him, 'You are the Christ'" (Mark 8:29).

THE SHELTER OF THE LORD

He who dwells in the shelter of the Most High will abide in the shadow of the Almighty. Psalm 91:1
Zion National Park, Utah, USA
Nikon D7000, ISO 125, f13.0, 1/50, Adobe Photoshop, Nik Silver Efex Pro
MYPHOTOWALK.COM—CATHERINEMARTIN.SMUGMUG.COM

DEVOTIONAL READING
BY OSWALD CHAMBERS

DEAR FRIEND,

The next two days are your opportunity to review what you have learned this week. You may wish to write your thoughts and insights in your Journal. As you think about your study of faith, write:

Your most significant insight:

Your favorite quote:

Your favorite verse:

Your most significant promise this week written in A Promise A Day:

Faith is a tremendously active principle which always puts Jesus Christ first— Lord, Thou hast said so and so (e.g., Matthew 6:33), it looks mad, but I am going to venture on Thy word. To turn head faith into a personal possession is a fight always, not sometimes. God brings us into circumstances in order to educate our faith, because the nature of faith is to make its object real.[14]

OSWALD CHAMBERS IN MY UTMOST FOR HIS HIGHEST

Viewer Guide
✒ WEEK ONE ✒

Faith In The Fourth Watch

You have just completed the first week of study in *Walk On Water Faith.* Today we are going to share together some devotional thoughts from Matthew 14:22-33. I want you to see how you can have faith in the fourth watch of the night when the wind is blowing hard in your life.

"And He said, 'Come!' And Peter got out of the boat, and walked on the water and came toward Jesus" (Matthew 14:29).

Devotional thoughts from Matthew 14:22-33 — How to have faith in the fourth watch:

1. _____ to Jesus.

2. _____ to Jesus.

3. _____ to Jesus.

Faith is taking God at His _____.

4. _____ Jesus.

Walk on water faith is the ability to see beyond temporal circumstances to the eternal realities of God and His _____, and as a result, take God at His Word and act on His _____ in spite of conflicting circumstances, thoughts, and feelings.

Never calculate a circumstance without _____.

5. _____ to Jesus.

6. _____ Jesus.

———

Video messages are available on DVDs or as Digital M4V Video. Audio messages are available as Digital MP3 Audio. Visit the Quiet Time Ministries Online Store at www.quiettime.org.

THE SCHOOL OF FAITH

The Gospels—Matthew, Mark, Luke, John

In the school of faith, sometimes we don't know what the lesson was until we've passed—or failed—the examination.[1]

WARREN WIERSBE

JESUS, YOUR TEACHER

When Jesus saw the crowds, He went up on the mountain; and after He sat down,
His disciples came to Him. He opened His mouth and began to teach them...

MATTHEW 5:1

PREPARE YOUR HEART

When you become a Christian and establish a forever relationship with the Lord, you enter the school of faith. The Lord takes you on as His disciple, a learner, and leads you on a unique journey of spiritual growth and maturity. Your spiritual maturity includes a growth in your faith (2 Corinthians 10:15, Romans 4:20). And there is great reward when you grow strong in faith. During our brief stay on earth, we have the privilege of a walk of faith. We enjoy an intimate, ongoing, vibrant relationship with Jesus. And one day, when we see our Lord face to face as we step from time into eternity, we will look forward to hearing those words, "Well done, good and faithful servant" (Matthew 25:23). Jesus is your teacher and the author and perfecter of your faith (Hebrews 12:2). He is serious about growing you into one who has a mature faith. He wants you to be strong and courageous and unshaken, not weak and shaking in fear. Again and again, He exhorted His disciples to not fear, not worry, and instead to trust and believe. And He will encourage the same character in you, transforming you into His faithful follower through the power of the Holy Spirit.

One servant of the Lord who matriculated in the school of faith was Mrs. Charles Cowman, beloved author of the best-selling *Streams in the Desert*. What many may not know is the story behind the writing of the book that has sustained and encouraged many a weary, suffering traveler in life. She and her husband, Charles, were missionaries in the Orient, founders of The Oriental Missionary Society, and teachers at the Bible Training Institute in Japan and Korea. They saw God work miracles as they worked with others helping place God's Word in 10,300,000 homes in villages in Japan. And then, Charles became ill, and these two active missionaries were forced to step back from their busy ministry into a secluded lifestyle. They experienced dark hours where their faith was challenged. Mrs. Cowman describes this difficult time: "Ah, a triumphant faith was needed just here. God gave it, and he found that it was possible to praise God in the darkest hour that ever swept a human life. If God were to give him songs in the night, He must first make it night…Charles Cowman stood still beneath the shadows of the Cross. It was my privilege to be by his side through six long pain-filled years. Often Satan came tempting us to faint under pressure, but each time when the temptings reached their utmost limit, God would illumine some old and familiar text, or a helpful book or tract would providentially fall into our hands which contained just the message needed at that moment."[2] She speaks fondly of the presence of their teacher, the Lord Jesus: "We caught anew a glimpse of His loving face. His choicest cordials were kept for our deepest faintings, and we were held in His strong loving arms throughout those years, till we learned to love our desert with its refreshing streams, because of His wonderful presence with us." Out of those desperate years in the school of faith came the collection of encouragements the Lord had given them, and it became *Streams in the Desert*.

Your time in the school of faith has already begun, dear friend. And you need to know that you are "His workmanship, created in Christ Jesus for good works, which God prepared beforehand" so that you will walk in them (Ephesians 2:10). This week is going to be a powerful time of study as you look at some of the most important principles of faith. As you begin this week learning all about the school of faith, ask God to speak to you and transform you by changing the way you think (Romans 12:2 NLT).

READ AND STUDY GOD'S WORD

1. Jesus was known as Teacher during the three years of His public ministry. In the gospels, He is referred to as "Rabbi" meaning "teacher" or "Rabboni" meaning "my teacher." A rabbi in Jesus' day interpreted the Torah, explained Scriptures, and told parables. Some traveled from one synagogue to another in different villages and took disciples with them. Jesus, however, was not a typical rabbi. He spoke with the authority of God. Following the Sermon on the Mount in Matthew 5-7, we discover that the crowd was "amazed at His teaching; for He was teaching them as one having authority, and not as their scribes" (Matthew 7:28-29). Look at the following verses and record what you observe about Him as teacher, how He taught, and about those who sat under His teaching and learned from Him.

Matthew 5:1-2

Matthew 8:1

Luke 9:43-48

Luke 10:1-2

Luke 10:38-42

Luke 11:1-10

2. Jesus emphasized the importance of His Word. Read the following verses and underline the most significant words and phrases for you today.

"Therefore, everyone who hears these words of Mine and acts on them, may be compared to a wise man who built his house on the rock. And the rain fell, and the floods came, and the winds blew and slammed against that house; and yet it did not fall, for it had been founded on the rock. Everyone who hears these words of Mine and does not act on them, will be like a foolish man who built his house on the sand. The rain fell, and the floods came, and the winds blew and slammed against that house; and it fell—and great was its fall." When Jesus had finished these words, the crowds were amazed at His teaching; for He was teaching them as one having authority, and not as their scribes.

MATTHEW 7:24-29

Heaven and earth will pass away, but My words will not pass away.

MATTHEW 24:35

If you continue in My word, then you are truly disciples of Mine; and you will know the truth, and the truth will make you free.

JOHN 8:3-32

I have given them Your word; and the world has hated them, because they are not of the world, even as I am not of the world. I do not ask You to take them out of the world, but to keep them from the evil one. They are not of the world, even as I am not of the world. Sanctify them in the truth; Your word is truth.

JOHN 17:14-17

3. Jesus invites you to enter His school of learning in Matthew 11:28-30. Read these verses and write out how are you encouraged to learn from Jesus. What will it take for you to sit at His feet each day to learn from Him?

ADORE GOD IN PRAYER

Be kind to your little children, Lord. Be a gentle teacher, patient with our weakness and stupidity. And give us the strength and discernment to do what You tell us, and so grow in Your likeness. May we all live in the peace that comes from You. May we journey towards Your city, sailing through the waters of sin untouched by the waves, borne serenely along by the Holy Spirit. Night and day may we give you praise and thanks, because You have shown us that all things belong to You, and all blessings are gifts from You. To You, the essence of wisdom, the foundation of truth, be glory for evermore.

CLEMENT OF ALEXANDRIA IN TO THE DIVINE TUTOR

YIELD YOURSELF TO GOD

Disciple is the word those who followed Jesus first received. Disciple means learner. They (the disciples) entered the school of faith and of life…Life is for learning, and there is no privilege greater than going to school. Christ is the Teacher, and we graduate into the High School of heaven to sit at His feet throughout eternity.

KEITH BROOKS IN SUMMARIZED BIBLE: COMPLETE SUMMARY OF THE NEW TESTAMENT

Faith is the eye by which we look to Jesus. A dimsighted eye is still an eye; a weeping eye is still an eye. Faith is the hand with which we lay hold of Jesus. A trembling hand is still a hand. And he is a believer whose heart within him trembles when he touches the hem of the Saviour's garment, that he may be healed. Faith is the tongue by which we taste how good the Lord is. A feverish tongue is nevertheless a tongue. And even then we may believe, when we are without the smallest portion of comfort; for our faith is founded not upon feelings, but upon the promises of God. Faith is the foot by which we go to Jesus. A lame foot is still a foot. He who comes slowly, nevertheless comes.[3]

GEORGE MUELLER

ENJOY HIS PRESENCE

Will you become a learner in the school of faith with your Teacher, Jesus, the author and perfecter of your faith? Will you sit at His feet and listen to His Word? If your faith is to grow, then you need to fuel it with the Word of God. "Faith comes from hearing, and hearing by the word of Christ" (Romans 10:17). The Lord will always bring you back to His Word, especially His promises, so you can know His "say-so" and respond with a resolve based on truth instead of living in the ever-changing waves of your circumstances and feelings. When you know the truth, the truth will indeed set you free (John 8:32). And oh, how you want to experience freedom in the Lord. You will be free to fly and dance on the water, above and through every difficulty, and close to Jesus. Pray the words of Psalm 25:4-5 as you close your quiet time today: "Make me know Your ways, O LORD; teach me Your paths. Lead me in Your truth and teach me, for You are the God of my salvation; for You I wait all the day." And ask God for His promise for you today and write it out in A Promise A Day.

REST IN HIS LOVE

"She had a sister called Mary, who was seated at the Lord's feet, listening to His word" (Luke 10:39).

THE GLORY OF CHRIST

And the Word became flesh, and dwelt among us, and we saw His glory. John 1:14
Zion National Park, Utah, USA
Nikon D7000, ISO 125, f22.0, 1/6, Adobe Photoshop, Nik Silver Efex Pro
MYPHOTOWALK.COM—CATHERINEMARTIN.SMUGMUG.COM

WHEN JESUS IS AMAZED

When Jesus heard this, He was amazed. Turning to the crowd that was following him, He said, "I tell you, I haven't seen faith like this in all Israel!"

LUKE 7:9

PREPARE YOUR HEART

Can you imagine the impact your faith has on the Lord? Are you aware of His constant presence and the fact that your actions can literally bring applause in heaven? The greatest example of this is the day a centurion made a request of Jesus. The centurion's encounter with Christ and his faith will be the subject of our study today.

Begin your quiet time with the words of this hymn by Lidie H. Edmunds, "My Faith Has Found a Resting Place."

My faith has found a resting place, not in a manmade creed;
I trust the ever living One, that He for me will plead.

Refrain
I need no other evidence, I need no other plea;
It is enough that Jesus died and rose again for Me.

Enough for me that Jesus saves, this ends my fear and doubt;
A sinful soul I come to Him, He will not cast me out. *Refrain*

My soul is resting on the Word, the living Word of God;
Salvation in my Savior's name, salvation through His blood. *Refrain*

The great Physician heals the sick, the lost He came to save;
For me His precious blood He shed, for me His life He gave. *Refrain*

READ AND STUDY GOD'S WORD

1. Oh what a day it was when a centurion sent a message to Jesus, asking Him to heal his servant who was ill. Read about this incredible experience in Luke 7:1-10 and write out what is most significant to you.

2. In Luke 7:9 we learn that when Jesus heard certain words from the centurion, "He marveled at him, and turned and said to the crowd that was following Him, 'I say to you, not even in Israel have I found such great faith.'" The New Living Translation translates it this way: "When Jesus heard this, He was amazed." Read the words of the centurion again in Luke 7:6-8 and write out why you think Jesus was amazed and why He called it a "great faith."

3. This centurion understood the principle of authority and realized that the words of Jesus are authoritative for all of life. He is the ultimate and only authority for our beliefs and actions. This is why one of the best definitions of faith is simply "taking God at His Word." When God says it, that settles it. The word of the Lord is all we need to know. Once we have His say-so, we can respond in faith. Always remember that "faith comes from hearing, and hearing by the word of Christ" (Romans 10:17). What do you learn about the attitude and actions of this centurion that you can apply to your own life? Have you made a firm decision about the authority of God's Word in your own life? Or do your circumstances and feelings have more authority for your actions?

4. Finally, look in Luke 7:7-8 at how the centurion reasoned through his situation and arrived at a decision of faith in sending that message to Jesus. Romans 12:2 says that you can be transformed by changing the way you think. Read Philippians 4:8 to learn the importance of your thoughts. How can God's promises in His Word help you think rightly, reason through a difficult circumstance by focusing on the truth, and arrive at great faith like the centurion?

5. Jesus is looking for faith (see Luke 18:8). Read the following promise in 2 Chronicles 16:9 and write out how these words from the Lord impact your faith in Him: "For the eyes of the LORD move to and fro throughout the earth that He may strongly support those whose heart is completely His."

ADORE GOD IN PRAYER

How does the centurion's faith inspire you to draw near and pour out your heart to the Lord today? Will you take some time to talk with Him about both your needs and desires? You may also wish to use your Prayer pages to write out special requests. Then, watch with eager expectation at how the Lord will respond to you. Remember that Jesus is the same yesterday, today and forever (Hebrews 13:8).

YIELD YOURSELF TO GOD

God is looking for men and women whose hearts are firmly fixed on Him and who will continually trust Him for all He desires to do with their lives. God is ready and eager to work more powerfully than ever through His people, and the clock of the centuries is striking the eleventh hour. The world is watching and waiting to see what God can do through a life committed to Him. And not only is the world waiting but God Himself awaits to see who will be the most devoted person who has ever lived: willing to be nothing so Christ may be everything; fully accepting God's purposes as his own; receiving Christ's humility, faith, love and power yet never hindering God's plan but always allowing Him to continue His miraculous work.

STREAMS IN THE DESERT

In the Word, the voice of God speaks to us directly. Every child of God is called to a direct intimate ongoing relationship with the Father, through the Word. As God reveals all His heart and grace in it, His child can, if he receives it from God, get all the life and power there is in the Word into his own heart and being…Every believer has the right and calling to stand in direct communication with God. It is in the Word God has revealed, it is in the Word He still reveals Himself to each individual…The Word is thus meant every day the means of the revelation of God Himself to the soul and of fellowship with Him. Have we learned to apply these truths? Do we understand that the Word ever says, "Seek God. Hearken to God. Wait for God. God will speak to you. Let God teach you?" All we hear about more Bible teaching and Bible study must lead to this one thing. We must be men and women, and we must help train others to be men and women, with whom the Word is never separated from the living God Himself, and who live as men and women to whom God in heaven speaks every day and all day.[4]

ANDREW MURRAY IN THE INNER LIFE

ENJOY HIS PRESENCE

Jesus is looking for faith-walking people just like the centurion. Faith-walking people pray. They attempt things well beyond their own strength. They are not daunted by feelings of despair and discouragement. When people tell them it's over, they know that God is on the move in their lives. When someone says they've reached the end of the road with a faith-walking person, they know it's not a setback but a new day. God is doing something greater than what they had in mind. Faith-walking people just don't give up. Hear it again. They don't give up! However, they may stop one thing in favor of another. Faith-walking people are simply not interested in short-sighted statements. They only want to know what God says, in His Word. They want to know what He promises and what He commands.

How has the faith of the centurion and Jesus' response impressed you today? Maybe you have reached that place where in your heart of hearts you have given up, withdrawn, stepped out of the race. The times became just too difficult and the dreams you once had are now gone. Today is a new day, dear friend. Jesus has a plan for your life. The Lord is calling out to you, saying, "Come." Will you walk on the water with Him? Close your quiet time by writing a prayer to the Lord expressing all that is on your heart. And be sure to write out your favorite promise today.

REST IN HIS LOVE

"I didn't even consider myself worthy to come to You. Just say the word, and my servant will be cured" (Luke 7:7).

HIS EYE IS ON YOU

I will counsel you with My eye upon you. Psalm 32:8
Zion National Park, Utah, USA
Nikon D7000, ISO 125, f13.0, 3 Bracketed EXP, Adobe Photoshop, Nik Silver Efex Pro
MYPHOTOWALK.COM—CATHERINEMARTIN.SMUGMUG.COM

WHEN YOUR FAITH GROWS

Turning to the disciples, He said privately, "Blessed are the eyes which see the things you see...
LUKE 10:23

PREPARE YOUR HEART

One of the great allegories is *Hinds Feet on High Places* by Hannah Hurnard about a young creature named Much Afraid who lived in the Valley of Humiliation. She is called to leave that low place and travel with the Good Shepherd who tenderly calls her to the High Places. She is given two companions, Sorrow and Suffering. The beauty of this story is that in spite of all the challenges she faces, she does arrive at her destination and is given a new name, Grace and Glory.

Real faith is exercised when we rely on Christ as our Savior, who died on the cross to pay for all our sins, and to give us the gift of eternal life. We learn in Ephesians 2:8-9 how we are saved: "By grace you have been saved through faith; and that not of yourselves, it is the gift of God; not as a result of works, so that no one may boast." All of us are given a measure of faith according to Romans 12:3. So have you ever put your faith in Christ? This faith decision may be expressed by a simple prayer: *Lord Jesus, I need You. Thank You for dying on the cross for my sins. I ask You now to come into My life, forgive my sins, and make me the person You want me to be.*

We live by our faith according Romans 1:17 where we are told, "The righteous man shall live by faith." The righteousness of God is revealed "from faith to faith" (Romans 1:17). Jesus is the author and perfecter of our faith (Hebrews12:2). As we are filled with the Holy Spirit (controlled and empowered), our faith grows and is more evident (Galatians 5:22). We can grow strong in faith and give great glory to God (Romans 4:20). And most importantly, when we come to know Christ by faith, something very powerful happens—we are "crucified with Christ"—and we say along with Paul, "it is no longer I who live, but Christ lives in me, and the life I now live in the flesh I live by faith in the Son of God who loved me and delivered Himself up for me" (Galatians 2:20). Christ is our life, and we depend on Him for everything, including our faith.

Faith is a gift from God (Romans 12:3) and can be exercised through reliance on Christ as He lives in us through the power of the Holy Spirit. That is why it is so important to be filled with the Spirit. Then you can say, along with Paul, "I can do all things through Him who strengthens me" (Philippians 2:13). So living and walking by faith is a journey of trust in Jesus, and we grow on that journey as our faith deepens through God's power and knowledge of His Word, including His magnificent promises. Faith is like a muscle that grows with use. We must indeed exercise our faith. When we step out in faith, taking God at His Word, relying on His promises, we are more likely to do it again, and again. Paul noted this kind of faith growth in the church at Thessalonica: "We must always thank God for you, brothers. This is right, since your faith is flourishing and the love each one of you has for one another is increasing. Therefore, we ourselves boast about you among God's churches—about your endurance and faith in all the persecutions and afflictions you endure" (2 Thessalonians 1:3-4 HCSB).

Where are you in this growth of faith? Have you received Jesus and established a relationship with God? If you have, then you are on the journey of growing in your faith. You are not who you were and yet, you are not who you will become as you grow. If you have not yet received Christ, then I invite you to pray a simple prayer like the one written above and begin the journey with Christ. Don't waste another minute to enter into the life of faith for it is truly a "fantastic adventure in trusting Him." Ask the Lord now, to speak to you as you spend time alone with Him today.

READ AND STUDY GOD'S WORD

1. Jesus took His disciples through many life experiences to show them His Person and power and to grow their faith. Read the following words of Jesus and experiences with Him and write out your thoughts about what Jesus was teaching the disciples and how He encouraged and challenged them in their faith. Note what they saw about Him and His mighty works.

Matthew 6:25-34

Matthew 14:13-21

Matthew 17:1-8, 17:14-21

Mark 11:22-23

Luke 10:21-24

2. Jesus taught His disciples about the Holy Spirit, who would be their Teacher, Helper, Comforter, and Power following His ascension into heaven. Read John 14:26, John 16:12-15, and Acts 1:8 and write what you learn about the Holy Spirit. The word for "power" in Acts 1:8 is *dunamis,* and is a power and strength that makes you able and capable.

3. In Ephesians 5:18 we learn that we are to "be filled with the Spirit." You can be filled with the Spirit by confessing any sin He reveals to you, and then asking Him by faith to fill you with His Spirit. When you are filled (controlled and empowered) by the Spirit, you will be controlled by Christ, and your life will exhibit the fruit of the Spirit, including faith/faithfulness. Read Galatians 5:22-25 and write about what will be seen in your life.

4. Your faith in God and His Word has amazing results. Read these verses and underline those words and verses most significant to you. Write in 1-2 words by each verse any results of faith you learn from that verse.

> If you continue in My word, then you are truly disciples of Mine; and You will know the truth, and the truth will make you free.
>
> JOHN 8:32

For whatever was written in earlier times was written for our instruction, so that through perseverance and the encouragement of the Scriptures we might have hope…Now may the God of hope fill you with all joy and peace in believing, so that you will abound in hope by the power of the Holy Spirit.

ROMANS 15:4, 13

For the word of the cross is foolishness to those who are perishing but to us who are being saved it is the power of God.

1 CORINTHIANS 1:18

While we look not at the things which are seen, but at the things which are not seen; for the things which are seen are temporal, but the things which are not seen are eternal.

2 CORINTHIANS 4:18

For we are His workmanship, created in Christ Jesus for good works, which God prepared beforehand so that we would walk in them.

EPHESIANS 2:10

ADORE GOD IN PRAYER

Pray these words from F.B. Meyer: "The mountain peaks of such a life as I desire to live call to me, yet they seem too steep and high for me to reach. But You know, Lord, and You have an infinite compassion for my weakness. Fulfill in me the good pleasure of Your will and the ideals you have taught me to cherish."[5]

YIELD YOURSELF TO GOD

Oswald Chambers writes about faith often in his devotional, *My Utmost For His Highest*. Meditate on these words to help in understanding how the Lord grows you in the life of faith: "God has frequently to knock the bottom board out of your experience if you are a saint in order to get you into contact with Himself. God wants you to understand that it is a life of faith, not a life of sentimental enjoyment of His blessings. Your earlier life of faith was narrow and intense, settled around a little sun-spot of experience that had as much of sense as of faith in it, full of light and sweetness; then God withdrew His conscious blessings in order to teach you to walk by faith."[6]

Oswald Chambers in My Utmost for His Highest

Enjoy His Presence

Think about a time when you took God at His Word and saw that your faith in God had grown. How do you need to grow in your faith? And how are you growing in your faith now and experiencing the results of freedom, hope, power, perspective, and purpose? Thank the Lord for how He is teaching you and ask Him to make you strong in Him with a "walk on water" type of faith that is bold and gets out of the boat with eyes firmly fixed on Him. Ask God for His promise in your life today from your quiet time with Him.

REST IN HIS LOVE

"Truly I say to you, if you have faith and do not doubt, you will not only do what was done to the fig tree, but even if you say to this mountain, 'Be taken up and cast into the sea,' it will happen" (Matthew 21:21).

ALL JOY AND PEACE

Now may the God of hope fill you with all joy and peace in believing. Romans 15:13
Zion National Park, Utah, USA
Nikon D7000, ISO 160, f11.0, 3 Bracketed EXP, Adobe Photoshop, Nik Silver Efex Pro

MYPHOTOWALK.COM—CATHERINEMARTIN.SMUGMUG.COM

WHEN YOUR FAITH IS TESTED

I have prayed for you, that your faith may not fail; and you when once you have turned again, strengthen your brothers.

LUKE 22:32

PREPARE YOUR HEART

George Mueller was once asked the best way to have strong faith. "The only way to learn strong faith is to endure great trials. I have learned my faith by standing firm amid severe testings," replied Mueller, a great hero of faith. A.B. Simpson wrote about the fear that threatens faith in the trial. He wrote, "If you are afraid, just look up and say, 'What time I am afraid I will trust in thee,' and you will yet thank God for the school of sorrow which was to you the school of faith." It's been said that great faith must have great trials. Another has said that "God's greatest gifts come through travail. Whether we look into the spiritual or temporal sphere, can we discover anything, any great reform, any beneficent discovery, any soul-awakening revival, which did not come through the toils and tears, the vigils and blood-shedding of men and women whose sufferings were the pangs of its birth?"[7]

The Bible speaks about tests of faith. These are the times when the truth of God and all He promises in His Word is challenged in our emotions and life circumstances. Trials are tests of faith for they challenge our belief in God's promises of power, His love, and His purpose for our lives. Do we believe that nothing is too hard for God? Do we believe Him when He says, "I have loved you with an everlasting love" (Jeremiah 31:3). Do we believe that He does have a plan for our welfare and not for calamity (Jeremiah 29:11)? Or are we afraid and ready to run for our very lives? We may easily have faith in these truths when the sun is shining, but what about when the storm of trouble rolls our way?

James, the brother of Jesus, acknowledged these tests of faith when he wrote, "Consider it all joy, my brethren, when you encounter various trials, knowing that the testing of your faith produces endurance. And let endurance have its perfect result, so that you may be perfect and complete, lacking in nothing" (James 1:3-4). Here we see that tests of faith actually make us stronger in our faith. Our endurance grows and we mature, and are able to walk through even more difficult trials.

We see these apparent tests of faith even in the Old Testament with the people of Israel during their 40 years wandering in the wilderness. Here is what God says about those times: "You shall remember all the way which the LORD your God has led you in the wilderness these forty years, that He might humble you, testing you, to know what was in your heart, whether you would keep His commandments or not. He humbled you and let you be hungry, and fed you with manna which you did not know, nor did your fathers know, that He might make you understand that man does not live by bread alone, but man lives by everything that proceeds out of the mouth of the LORD" (Deuteronomy 8:2-3). Living by the words of God is another way of saying that He wanted them to understand how to walk and live by faith. And the school of faith includes humbling, testing, learning, submission and surrender.

Are you being tested right now? Get ready for new growth in your faith, a greater view of God, and a deeper experience of power in God's promises. How is your trust in God and His Word being challenged? Ask the Lord to speak to you today and to encourage your faith.

READ AND STUDY GOD'S WORD

1. When Jesus trained the twelve disciples, He taught them many lessons on faith. One lesson occurred in a boat on the Sea of Galilee. Read Matthew 8:18-28 (see also Luke 8:22-25). Think about the following questions and write your insights:

What were the orders, the words of Jesus, in Matthew 8:18?

What happened to test the disciples' faith in those words?

How did the disciples respond and what did they say?

What did Jesus say about their response and what did He do?

2. What do you think the disciples learned that day on the Sea of Galilee? How do you think that experience helped grow their faith?

3. Jesus spoke with Peter one day about a time when his faith would be challenged and tested. Read the following verses and write out what you learn about Jesus' care and concern for your faith.

Luke 22:31-34

Luke 22:54-62

John 21:4-19

4. In the great tests of our faith, we are challenged with the temptation of unbelief. Unbelief is one of the greatest hindrances to faith. The Greek word for unbelief is *apistia* and means *uncertainty, distrust, weakness in faith, and faithlessness.* Read Mark 9:14-29 about a father whose faith was tested with a son who was demon-possessed. What was his prayer? What do you learn about the importance of prayer from the example of the disciples in this situation when you are tempted with unbelief?

5. Describe a time when your own faith was tested. What did you learn and how did you grow? What promise in God's Word became more significant to you during that time?

6. Read this amazing promise from Job 23:10 and underline your favorite phrase and truth to encourage you today: "He knows the way that I take; when He has tested me, I will come forth as gold."

ADORE GOD IN PRAYER

Turn to your Prayer pages in the back of this book and write out your deep heart prayer needs to the Lord. Be sure to date each request so you can return to see how God answers each prayer. Be encouraged from the words of David, "In the morning, O LORD, You will hear my voice; in the morning I will order my prayer to You and eagerly watch" (Psalm 5:3)

YIELD YOURSELF TO GOD

Our Father does not test our faith so much as He exercises and develops it. In time, He makes us aware of our utter weakness; and, in time, we trust and rest in His all-sufficient strength. "Until we are carried quite out of our depth, beyond all our own wisdom and resources, we are no more than beginners in the school of faith. Only as everything fails us and we fail ourselves, do we draw upon abiding strength. 'Blessed is the man whose strength is in Thee'; not partly in Thee and partly in himself. The devil often makes men strong, strong in themselves to do evil—great conquerors, great acquirers of wealth and power. The Lord on the contrary makes His servant weak, puts him in circumstances that will show him his nothingness, that he may lean upon the strength that is unfailing. It is a long lesson for most of us, but it cannot be passed over until deeply learned. And God Himself thinks no trouble too great, no care too costly to teach us this. Faith counts on the Word of God outside and apart from everything and everyone here. When you are in faith your life is centered in the Lord Jesus."[8]

MILES J. STANFORD AND J.B.S. IN COMPLETE WORKS OF MILES J. STANFORD

God moves in a mysterious way, His wonders to perform; He plants His footsteps in the sea, and rides upon the storm.

WILLIAM COWPER IN OLNEY HYMNS

Hard places are the very school of faith and character…dear suffering child of God, you cannot fail if only you dare to believe, to stand fast and refuse to be overcome.

MRS. CHARLES COWMAN IN STREAMS IN THE DESERT

When He (God) gave you promises and asked you to trust them, He made His promises suitable for times of storms and high seas…We have all seen swords that are beautiful but are useless in war, or shoes made for decoration but not for walking. Yet God's shoes are made of iron and brass, and we can walk all the way to heaven in them, without ever wearing them out. And we could swim the Atlantic a thousand times in His life vest, with no fear of ever sinking. His Word of promise is meant to be tried and tested…O beloved, I plead with you not to treat God's promises as something to be displayed in a museum but to use them as everyday sources of comfort. And whenever you have a time of need, trust the Lord.

CHARLES HADDON SPURGEON IN STREAMS IN THE DESERT

ENJOY HIS PRESENCE

What is your most significant insight from your quiet time today? What lesson from the school of faith can you take with you that will help you to walk on water with your faith no matter what you experience in life? And what is your promise from the Lord that you can write out and then carry with you through the day?

REST IN HIS LOVE

"Consider it all joy, my brethren, when you encounter various trials, knowing that the testing of your faith produces endurance" (James 1:3).

MORE PRECIOUS THAN GOLD

Your faith is more precious than mere gold. 1 Peter 1:7 NLT

Zion National Park, Utah, USA

Nikon D7000, ISO 160, f11.0, 3 Bracketed EXP, Adobe Photoshop, Nik Silver Efex Pro
MYPHOTOWALK.COM—CATHERINEMARTIN.SMUGMUG.COM

THE SHOUT OF FAITH

Father, if You are willing, take this cup away from Me—
nevertheless, not My will, but Yours, be done.
Luke 22:42 HCSB

PREPARE YOUR HEART

At the age of fifty-four, Mrs. Charles Cowman had to drink a cup of suffering she did not desire. Her precious husband went to heaven and she was now a widow. She wrote in her journal: "I must look at the glory side. I must think of Charlie's joy." They had always been together and this was a new journey. She reasoned that the more lonely she was, the sweeter would be her fellowship with Christ. She described the time as an aloneness that made her feel like a wandering bird out of its nest. She determined to follow the Lord's way and not her own. She did not feel like writing, but sensed the Lord desired her to write her husband's biography. She prayed, "God, hold my lonely heart in Thy loving hand." Ultimately she surrendered with the great shout of faith, "Thy will be done." She did not view life in terms of circumstances, but in light of the Lord. He Himself was her Circumstance. How could she arrive at this conclusion? She had the say-so of God in written form in His Word and she clung to it. Mrs. Cowman, strengthened by the Lord, was able to write *Charles E. Cowman, Missionary Warrior*, the biography of her precious husband. Though she did not desire the season of aloneness, she received it from the Lord's hand, and spent the next thirty-six years serving the Lord as a writer on the mission field.

Suffering comes in many forms. It may be a loss of a loved one, a change in job, aging, illness, financial challenges, rejection, failure, death of a dream, and more. When we are handed a cup of suffering, we are led to a new surrender where we receive all from the hand of the Lord. We discover that the Lord's ways are higher than our ways (Isaiah 55:8-9) and that He is asking us to trust Him though we do not understand His plan (Proverbs 3;5-6). In the midst of drinking the cup, there comes the day when we shout a great shout of faith in utter surrender. Job, in his suffering, after losing almost everything, cried out, "Though He slay me, I will hope in Him" (Job 13:15). Jesus cried out in prayer in the Garden of Gethsemane, "Father, if you are willing, take this cup away from Me—nevertheless, not My will, but Yours, be done" (Luke 22:42 HCSB). During His suffering, while hanging on the cross, He cried again to His Father, "My God, My God, why have You forsaken Me?" (Mark 15:34). His ultimate cry of faith came, when Jesus cried out from the cross just before He breathed His last breath, " Father, into Your hands I commit My Spirit" (Luke 23:46). And the apostle Paul cried out upon realizing his thorn in the flesh would remain, "Most gladly, therefore, I will rather boast about my weaknesses, so that the power of Christ may dwell in me" (2 Corinthians 12:9). In the school of faith, sometimes we are asked to drink from a cup of suffering. And the shout of faith comes in the strength and power of the Lord at work in us when we say "yes" to the Lord and His will. Jesus says, "In the world you have tribulation, but take courage; I have overcome the world" (John 16:33). Today, as you look at how you can say "yes" in obedience to the Lord by faith, even in the heat of a trial, ask the Lord to speak to you from His Word.

READ AND STUDY GOD'S WORD

1. Jesus trained His twelve disciples for three years in public ministry. He was popular and drew large crowds whenever He taught. The religious authorities of the day plotted to have Him arrested and killed. What they did not realize is that their actions played into the sovereign plan of God. For in Isaiah 53 we see that the Messiah would bear our griefs and carry our sorrows. And here are the words that reveal the truth that the Lord's ways are higher than our ways: "But the LORD was pleased to crush Him, putting Him to grief; if He would render Himself as a guilt offering, He will see His offspring…My Servant will justify the many, and He will bear their iniquities" (Isaiah 53:10-12). And so, we clearly see that Jesus knew what was ahead before He went to the Garden of Gethsemane to pray to His Father. He knew He would be arrested, scourged, and ultimately crucified, to pay for our sins, intercede for us, and give us the gift of eternal life, all in God the Father's plan. Read Matthew 26:36-46 and write your most significant insight from the example of Jesus in the face of great suffering. Think especially about what He prayed and how He prayed.

2. In Hebrews 5:7-8 we learn more about the example of Jesus in the depth of His suffering. Write out what you learn from Jesus about prayer and obedience. Then, write your thoughts about why prayer and obedience are expressions of faith.

3. Jesus learned obedience from the things He suffered (Hebrews 5:8). What does that mean, since He was already obedient and never disobedient? Obedience is *hupakoe* in the Greek and is *the faith which obeys God's will*. We see in Hebrews 5:8 that Jesus endured the difficult experience of obedience in the heat of the things He suffered. In fact, Philippians 2:8 tells us that He humbled Himself by becoming obedient to the point of death, even death on a cross. This obedience in suffering was the supreme expression of faith. We see that faith requires obedience. Read Romans 1:1-6 and Romans 16:25-27 and write what you learn about the obedience of faith.

4. Jesus is the great example of faith for us, as He was utterly dependent on the Father and surrendered to God's plan and purpose. Now, as you think about your own dependence on the Lord, read John 15:1-5 and write out what the Lord is asking of you. The word *abide* is *meno* in the Greek and means *to remain in vital contact with Jesus*. Note especially how He says, "apart from Me you can do nothing" (John 15:5). That means you need Jesus—He is the source of everything including your faith. How important are His words in John 15:1-5 for your ability to walk by faith?

5. Jesus has made faith possible because He lives in you through the power of the Holy Spirit. You can shout the shout of faith because of Christ's provision of His very life in you. Read Galatians 2:20 and Ephesians 5:18 and write out what you learn about how Jesus provides for your faith. (As you learned in Day 3, to be filled with the Spirit means to be controlled and empowered by Christ Himself).

6. In the school of faith, there are five important passages from God's Word—great promises—that will strengthen your faith especially when you need a shout of faith in the face of great

suffering. The truths will encourage you to surrender to the Lord and trust Him no matter what. Read these passages in and underline your favorite words and phrases.

> Trust in the LORD with all your heart and do not lean on your own understanding. In all your ways acknowledge Him, and He will make your paths straight.
>
> PROVERBS 3:5-6

> "For My thoughts are not your thoughts, nor are your ways My ways," declares the LORD. "For as the heavens are higher than the earth, so are My ways higher than your ways and My thoughts than your thoughts. For as the rain and the snow come down from heaven, and do not return there without watering the earth and making it bear and sprout, and furnishing seed to the sower and bread to the eater; so will My word be which goes forth from My mouth; it will not return to Me empty, without accomplishing what I desire, and without succeeding in the matter for which I sent it."
>
> ISAIAH 55:8-11

> For God so loved the world, that He gave His only begotten Son, that whoever believes in Him shall not perish, but have eternal life.
>
> JOHN 3:16

> Be anxious for nothing, but in everything by prayer and supplication with thanksgiving let your requests be made known to God. And the peace of God, which surpasses all comprehension, will guard your hearts and your minds in Christ Jesus.
>
> PHILIPPIANS 4:6-7

> For we do not have a high priest who cannot sympathize with our weaknesses, but One who has been tempted in all things as we are, yet without sin. Therefore let us draw near with confidence to the throne of grace, so that we may receive mercy and find grace to help in time of need.
>
> HEBREWS 4:15-16

7. What have you learned today that will encourage you to trust the Lord by faith in the heat of a trial you don't understand?

ADORE GOD IN PRAYER

Father, I abandon myself into Your hands;

do with me what You will.

Whatever you may do, I thank You:

I am ready for all, I accept all.

Let only Your will be done in me, and in

all Your creatures—I wish no more than this, O Lord.

CHARLES DE FOUCAULD PRAYER OF ABANDONMENT

YIELD YOURSELF TO GOD

"My Father, if it is possible, let this cup pass me by" (Matthew 26:39). Jesus couldn't face it. Too much pain to hold, too much suffering to embrace, too much agony to live through. He didn't feel he could drink that cup filled to the brim with sorrows. Why then could he still say yes? I can't fully answer that question, except to say that beyond all the abandonment experienced in body and mind Jesus still had a spiritual bond with the one he called Abba. He possessed a trust beyond betrayal, a surrender beyond despair, a love beyond all fears. This intimacy beyond all intimacies made it possible for Jesus to allow the request to let the cup pass him by become a prayer directed to the one who had called him "My Beloved." Notwithstanding his anguish, that bond of love had not been broken. It couldn't be felt in the body, nor thought through in the mind. But it was there, beyond all feelings and thoughts, and it maintained the communion underneath all disruptions. It was that spiritual sinew, that intimate communion with his Father, that made him hold on to the cup and pray: "My Father, let it be as you, not I, would have it" (Matthew 26:39).[9]

HENRI NOUWEN IN CAN YOU DRINK THE CUP

Faith is the communication link between heaven and earth. It is on this link of faith that God's messages of love travel so quickly that even before we ask, He answers. And while we are still speaking, "He hears us" (1 John 5:14)…faith honors God and God honors faith.

STREAMS IN THE DESERT

Faith by its very nature must be tried and the real trial of faith is not that we find it difficult to trust God, but that God's character has to be cleared in our minds. Faith in its actual working out has to go through spells of unsyllabled isolation… Faith in the Bible is faith in God against everything that contradicts Him—I will remain true to God's character whatever He may do. "Though He slay me, yet I will trust Him"—this is the most sublime utterance of faith in the whole of the Bible.[10]

OSWALD CHAMBERS IN MY UTMOST FOR HIS HIGHEST

ENJOY HIS PRESENCE

Where in your life do you need to trust the Lord even though you don't understand His plan? God's plan accomplishes so much more than we can ask or imagine. Do you sense His active presence in your life and will you draw nearer to Him and grow deeper in your faith? Will you surrender to the Lord's ways and plans and trust Him when you are tried in your faith? Will you abide in Christ, and rely on Him for everything in your life, including faith in His provision? And finally, will you pray? Prayer means you believe God hears and will answer your cries. So pour out your heart to the Lord, and shout the shout of faith, dear friend, following the great example of Jesus. Write out your most significant insight, and then carry that thought with you throughout the day. Write your favorite promise in A Promise A Day.

REST IN HIS LOVE

"Trust in the LORD with all your heart, and do not rely on your own understanding; think about Him in all your ways, and He will guide you on the right paths" (Proverbs 3:5-6 HCSB).

COMING FORTH AS GOLD

When He has tried me, I shall come forth as gold. Job 23:10
Zion National Park, Utah, USA
Nikon D7000, ISO 160, f11.0, 3 Bracketed EXP, Adobe Photoshop, Nik Silver Efex Pro
MYPHOTOWALK.COM—CATHERINEMARTIN.SMUGMUG.COM

DEVOTIONAL READING
BY MRS. CHARLES COWMAN

DEAR FRIEND,

This week has been a deep time of study and learning about walk on water faith. Take some time now to write about all that you have learned this week. What have you learned about the school of faith that will help you have the kind of faith that walks on water, standing strong and courageous, and marching triumphantly in the storms of life? What has been most significant to you? Close by writing a prayer to the Lord.

What were your most meaningful discoveries this week as you spent time with the Lord?

Most meaningful insight:

Most meaningful devotional reading:

Most meaningful verse:

Your most significant promise this week written in A Promise A Day:

As you think about all that you have learned this week, meditate on these words by Mrs. Charles Cowman:

The way was long, and the shadows spread far as the eye could see.

I stretched my hands to a human Christ, who walked through the night with me.

Out of the darkness we came at last, our feet on the dawn-warm sod,

And I knew by the light in His wondrous eye, that I walked with the Son of God.

MRS. CHARLES COWMAN IN SPRINGS IN THE VALLEY

Viewer Guide
❦ WEEK TWO ❦

Faith That Amazes Jesus

In our time together in this message, we are going to look at the true story in Luke 7 about a centurion who had such great faith that Jesus was amazed. Our goal is to discover what it was about his faith that was so great.

"When Jesus heard this, he was amazed at him, and turning to the crowd following him, he said, 'I tell you, I have not found such great faith even in Israel" (Luke 7:9 NIV).

Amazed — to wonder, marvel, be struck with admiration or astonishment.

Two places where Jesus is amazed — Luke 7:9 and Mark 6:6

At great _____ or great _____.

What will lead you to great faith?

Acting solely on the _____ of God's Word. Luke 7:8

What happens when we surrender to God and His Word as the authority for our belief, so that it commands our beliefs and actions?

1. Our hearts are _____. Psalm 119:50

2. We see _____. John 5:39

3. We are _____for every good work. 2 Timothy 3:16-17

4. Our _____ are pierced, and the Word judges our thoughts and intentions. Hebrews 4:12

5. We experience the _____ and purposes of God. Isaiah 55:10-11

6. We know what is _____. John 17:17

7. We are given _____. Romans 15:4

8. The Word gives us _____ for our path. Psalm 119:105

What are five ways you can grow in your love for God's Word?

1. Make _____ with God and His Word
a priority.

2. Have more than one Bible reading _____for your quiet time.

3. _____the Word in your Quiet Time Journal or Quiet Time
Notebook.

4. _____ through the promises.

5. _____ God's promises.

❧ *Video messages are available on DVDs or as Digital M4V Video. Audio messages are available as Digital MP3 Audio. Visit the Quiet Time Ministries Online Store at www.quiettime.org.*

Week Three
THE GALLERY OF FAITH

Hebrews 11

Your course, through grace, is one of faith, and sight seldom cheers you; this has also been the pathway of the brightest and the best. Faith was the orbit in which these stars of the first magnitude moved all the time of their shining here.[1]

CHARLES HADDON SPURGEON

WHAT YOU NEED WHEN FEAR SETS IN

*Remember those who led you, who spoke the word of God to you; and
considering the result of their conduct, imitate their faith.*

HEBREWS 13:7

PREPARE YOUR HEART

Have you ever experienced a time when a storm came into your life and it just seemed to last forever? The wind kept raging. The rain kept falling. And then, just when you thought you had seen the end of the trial, another challenge comes your way. David, the man after God's own heart, experienced just such an adversity when he was chased by Saul, the most powerful man on earth. David had the promise from God that he would someday be king. But that "someday" seemed like an impossibility because of the danger. Perhaps he was afraid he would never see the light of the promise he had from the Lord. He responded by crying out to God, "How long, O LORD? Will You forget me forever? How long will You hide Your face from me?" (Psalm 13:1). The good news is that God carried David through that trial and fulfilled the promise to be king. David is one encouraging example for you in the heat of your own prolonged challenging circumstance, whatever it may be.

There is such hope in examples of others who have survived triumphantly and walked by faith in impossible circumstances. God encourages you in Hebrews 13:7 to "remember those who led you, who spoke the word of God to you; and considering the result of their conduct, imitate their faith." This week you are going to have the opportunity to build a long list of examples of faith to remember, consider, and imitate. Hebrews 11 has been called the Gallery of Faith and The Hall of Fame of Faith. It is probably one of the most important chapters in the Bible when it comes to studying and understand faith.

Hebrews is not a letter, but a sermon in written form. The author is unnamed but was clearly known to his audience. He is writing his words to encourage those dear to him to not give up. Hebrews is written for people who have grown tired in the race, have become afraid and timid, and need encouragement in faith and refreshment with new vision for the days ahead. Can you relate to their challenges in life? Are you needing that same kind of encouragement and vision just now? Then get ready for a week of quiet times in Hebrews 11, The Gallery of Faith, also known by many as The Hall of Fame of Faith, to help you run your race.

Take some time now to draw near to the Lord and write a prayer, asking Him to speak to your heart.

READ AND STUDY GOD'S WORD

1. This week you are going to live in Hebrews 11, one of the great chapters in the Bible on faith. The context for Hebrews 11 is discouragement, fatigue, and fear. The book of Hebrews is filled with strong exhortations—encouragements designed to promote faith in a great and mighty God. Read the following verses in Hebrews as a study in context, and underline the words and phrases that help you understand the struggles of these believers and that also encourage your own faith.

> Let us hold fast the confession of our hope without wavering for He who promised is faithful; and let us consider how to stimulate one another to love and good deeds.
>
> HEBREWS 10:23-24

> But remember the former days, when, after being enlightened, you endured a great conflict of sufferings.
>
> HEBREWS 10:32

> Therefore, do not throw away your confidence, which has a great reward. For you have need of endurance, so that when you have done the will of God, you may receive what was promised.
>
> HEBREWS 10:35-36

Therefore, since we have so great a cloud of witnesses surrounding us, let us also lay aside every encumbrance and the sin which so easily entangles us, and let us run with endurance the race that is set before us, fixing our eyes on Jesus, the author and perfecter of faith, who for the joy set before Him endured the cross, despising the shame, and has sat down at the right hand of the throne of God. For consider Him who has endured such hostility by sinners against Himself, so that you will not grow weary and lose heart.

HEBREWS 12:1-3

2. Hebrews seems to be written to a people who were in a *then* and *now* situation. *Then*, when they experienced trials, they had been faithful. They had grasped God's promise and walked by faith. *Now*, they were experiencing another, possibly more powerful storm, and they were afraid. They needed to once again live by faith in God's promises, and grow strong in confidence and endurance. So, the writer of Hebrews, knowing the power of example, marches past his readers a long, wonderful list of those who have been faithful to the Lord. He wants them to see "a living faith which acts in terms of God's promises, even when the realization of the promise is not in sight. Such a dynamic faith is able to move beyond disappointments and the sufferings experienced in this world and to bear a ringing testimony to future generations of the reality in the promised blessings."[2]

Take some time now to read through Hebrews 11. In Hebrews 11:4 we learn that those who walk by faith have lives that can speak to us today. After you have read Hebrews 11, write in 1-2 sentences how these lives speak to you today.

3. Who has been a living example for you with the kind of faith that you can imitate?

ADORE GOD IN PRAYER

Pray the prayer of Corrie ten Boom today remembering that God loves you and has strength and power for you today. He promises in His Word. And that is the fuel for your faith.

> "Father, thank You for Your Word,
>   which tells us over and over again
>   that You know each one of us
>   who is Your child
>   and that you also know all our needs."[3]

YIELD YOURSELF TO GOD

What then can we say about Hebrews today? Hebrews is a sermon that is rooted in real life. It addresses men and women like ourselves who discover that they can be penetrated by circumstances over which they have no control. It is a sensitive response to the emotional fragileness that characterizes each one of us. It throbs with an awareness of struggle as it explores the dimensions of the cost of discipleship. Hebrews is a pastoral response to the sagging faith of frightened men and women at a time when the imperial capital was striving to regain its composure after the devastation of the great fire. It conveys a word from God addressed to the harsh reality of life in an insecure world. If you have ever felt yourself overwhelmed by that reality, Hebrews is a sermon you cannot afford to neglect.[4]

WILLIAM LANE IN HEBREWS, A CALL TO COMMITMENT

ENJOY HIS PRESENCE

How are you encouraged today from these examples to move beyond fear to faith, and step away from discouragement towards confidence and endurance? What is your favorite promise from the Lord? Write it in A Promise A Day. Then, take a few moments to reflect on the devotional photo in today's quiet time. Stand strong, dear friend. There is more encouragement to come from Hebrews 11.

REST IN HIS LOVE

"Therefore, do not throw away your confidence, which has a great reward. For you have need of endurance, so that when you have done the will of God, you may receive what was promised." (Hebrews 10:35-36).

ETERNAL WEIGHT OF GLORY

An absolutely incomparable eternal weight of glory. 2 Corinthians 4:17 HCSB
Zion National Park, Utah, USA
Nikon D7000, ISO 640, f4.5, 1/125, Adobe Photoshop, Nik Silver Efex Pro
MYPHOTOWALK.COM—CATHERINEMARTIN.SMUGMUG.COM

FINDING A FAITH THAT PLEASES GOD

*And without faith it is impossible to please Him, for he who comes to God
must believe that He is and that He is a rewarder of those who seek Him.*

HEBREWS 11:6

PREPARE YOUR HEART

Florence, Italy is the heart of the Renaissance where magnificent works of art may be seen even today. One of the most magnificent places in Florence is the Uffizi Gallery. Some of the great artists of the Renaissance are Michelangelo, Raphael, Leonardo da Vinci, Botticelli, Donatello, and Titian. When you walk the halls of the Uffizi Gallery, you will see paintings you have perhaps heard of if you had the opportunity to study art history in school. As you walk through Rooms 10-14 you will gaze at "The Birth of Venus" by Botticelli. Room 15 is dedicated to paintings by Leonardo da Vinci. Room 25 contains Michelangelo's "Holy Family." A new appreciation for the beauty and magnificence of art grows as you see painting after painting by the masters of the Renaissance.

But there is a gallery that God has filled — not with art — but with people. God desires that you walk through His Gallery of Faith, and study each person to understand the kind of faith He wants you to have. This kind of faith pleases Him and will help you run your race in life and cross the finish line.

Now, as you are about to enter God's Gallery of Faith, take some time to ask Him to speak to you, showing you exactly what He wants you to see. Write a prayer to Him expressing all that is on your heart.

READ AND STUDY GOD'S WORD

1. We are about to enter God's amazing Gallery of Faith. Imagine that you are in the finest art gallery you've ever seen. And just before you enter the magnificent gallery, there is important information that will help you understand what you are going to see. As we are about to enter the Gallery of Faith, and look at some of the finest and most memorable examples of faith, we need to stop and read the opening words of Hebrews 11:1-6. Read these first six verses and write out everything you learn about faith.

2. Hebrews 11:1 gives us a great definition of faith: "Now faith is the assurance of things hoped for, the conviction of things not seen." Assurance is *hupostasis* in the Greek and means a firm, confident foundation. Conviction is *elegchos* in the Greek and means proof of something that is true. William Lane describes Hebrews 11:1 as "a statement that sums up all the preacher wanted to affirm about the intensity and capacity of faith…it celebrates the objective reality of the blessings for which we hope, the demonstration of events as yet unseen…faith provides the objective ground upon which Christians may base their subjective confidence. It is this capacity of faith that allows Christians to maintain a firm grasp upon truth…in the knowledge that the blessings for which they hope are guaranteed by the promise of God."[5] With this in mind, how does Hebrews 11:1 help you understand faith more?

3. Read Hebrews 11:6 and write out what is necessary for a faith that pleases God.

4. How can you increase your knowledge of who God is and what God does?

5. Wuest in his *Word Studies* defines faith this way: "Faith apprehends as a real fact what is not revealed to the senses. It rests on that fact, acts upon it, and is upheld by it in the face of all that seems to contradict it. Faith is real seeing."[6] Think about all you've learned in Hebrews 11:1-6, Wuest's definition, and the short definition of faith as "taking God at His Word" and the longer definition of "Faith is the ability to see beyond temporal circumstances to the eternal realities of God and His promises, and as a result, take God at His Word and act on His promises in spite of conflicting circumstances, thoughts, and feelings." Now, write out in your own words what faith is.

ADORE GOD IN PRAYER

Pray the prayer by F.B. Meyer to the Lord today: "Most gracious God, make me alive by your Holy Spirit, I pray, that I may run in the way marked out for me, with earnest desire. Give me preparedness and alertness, and may I ever keep looking to Jesus."[7]

YIELD YOURSELF TO GOD

> Faith is the sixth sense. It makes us as sure of unseen or future things, which we know about only through the divine Word, as we are of things which we can see and touch. When we are aware of the reality of these things, we naturally take them into account when we act.[8]
>
> F.B. MEYER IN THE DEVOTIONAL COMMENTARY

ENJOY HIS PRESENCE

What is the most important truth you have learned about faith today? And what if your favorite promise (write in A Promise A Day).

REST IN HIS LOVE

"Faith is the confidence that what we hope for will actually happen; it gives us assurance about things we cannot see" (Hebrews 11:1 NLT).

REACHING FOR THE PRIZE

I press on toward the goal for the prize. Philippians 3:14
Zion National Park, Utah, USA
Nikon D7000, ISO 125, f13.0, 1/125, Adobe Photoshop, Nik Silver Efex Pro
MYPHOTOWALK.COM—CATHERINEMARTIN.SMUGMUG.COM

IMITATING THE ACTIONS OF FAITH

By faith Noah, being warned by God about things not yet seen, in reverence prepared an ark for the salvation of his household, by which he condemned the world, and became an heir of the righteousness which is according to faith.

HEBREWS 11:7

PREPARE YOUR HEART

Actions speak louder than words. A person may say they believe something is true, but if they don't act on it, the words are just talk. If someone told you that they had just deposited a large sum of money in your bank account as a gift to you, what would be your first response? At first, you might laugh. But if the person was a credible friend or someone you knew had the means to give such a gift, then you might begin to believe it was true. If they handed you a checkbook, would you just file it away and go about living your life? No! You would check the account, and if you believed the balance was true, then you would start writing checks on the account.

In the same way, God has given you a full account of promises in His Word. He stands behind every promise and you can launch out in faith on the authority of God and His Word. Knowing His Word is true, will prompt us to take action based on His promises.

Amy Carmichael was one person who knew God could be trusted. Her action included leaving the safety and security of home to serve her Lord in India, helping rescue young girls from temple prostitution. She took action based on the promise that God was leading her and would provide for her every step of the way.

Hebrews 11 is filled with examples of men and women of God who believed Him and took action based on His promises to them. Today you are going to look at those actions and learn about the kinds of things God's people of faith do in response to His Word. You will see the power of God that comes from faith in His promises. Will you pray today and ask God to make you a person of faith who will take action based on His promise, His say-so to you?

Read and Study God's Word

1. Today you are going to walk through God's Gallery of Faith and look at each person, studying their actions. Read Hebrews 11 and write out all the actions of each person of faith using just a few words of description. For example, in Hebrews 11:7 we see that Noah, in reverence, prepared an ark. You may use a Journal page if you need more space. God bless you as you live in His Word today.

2. What is the most important truth you learned in your study today?

ADORE GOD IN PRAYER

Talk with God now, pouring out your heart, and ask Him to help you know the actions of faith necessary in your own life. Ask Him to open up His Word to you and give you promises to hold on to today.

YIELD YOURSELF TO GOD

> The life of faith is like a ladder up to heaven which twists and turns, and appears not to be fastened to anything. It seems to hang in the air, and you see no further than the step on which you are standing. The next step seems to go out into an abyss, into oblivion, yet when you take it you find yourself upon a rock. Occasionally the clouds part before you, and then you catch a glimpse of the King in His glory, so eagerly you pick yourself up and go on. When you look back you are amazed as you realize how God has led. His voice is always saying, "Forward, Onward, Upward!"[9]
>
> ALAN REDPATH IN FAITH FOR THE TIMES

ENJOY HIS PRESENCE

Dear friend, today God is speaking to you in His Word. You walked through His Gallery of Faith and saw men and women of action. How were you inspired and challenged? What is God teaching you and how is He encouraging you? What is His promise for your today?

REST IN HIS LOVE

"And what more shall I say? For time will fail me if I tell of Gideon, Barak, Samson, Jephthah, of David and Samuel and the prophets, who by faith conquered kingdoms, performed acts of righteousness, obtained promises, shut the mouths of lions..." (Hebrews 11:32-33).

TRUST IN HIM AT ALL TIMES

Trust in Him at all times, O people; Pour out your heart before Him. Psalm 62:8
Zion National Park, Utah, USA
Nikon D7000, ISO 160, f22.0, 1/10, Adobe Photoshop, Nik Silver Efex Pro
MYPHOTOWALK.COM—CATHERINEMARTIN.SMUGMUG.COM

OVERCOMING THE TESTS OF FAITH

By faith Abraham, when he was called, obeyed by going out to a place which he was
to receive for an inheritance; and he went out, not knowing where he was going.

HEBREWS 11:8

PREPARE YOUR HEART

When God gives you His Word, you can count on it. However, there will most likely be aspects of your temporal circumstances that will challenge the actions of faith in His Word. During World War II, a man who was a soldier on duty in France, described a time of fear and discouragement. He wondered how he could make it. He felt weak and alone. A Chaplain in his area arranged a church service in one of the small chapels. The soldier attended. Softly the organ played the music, and they sang the words of the hymn, "Be still my soul; the Lord is on Thy side." Oh how desperately this man needed to hear these promises from God's Word for he felt so alone. The second stanza encouraged him even more. "Be still my soul; the Lord doth undertake to guide the future as He hath the past." The man realized the truth in God's Word that God is sovereign and in control. He was encouraged to never give up.

Oh how the promises of God can encourage you and strengthen you when your faith is tested. When you are tempted to believe circumstances and feelings that challenge the Word of God, then your faith is being tested. In Hebrews 11, every man or woman experienced a challenge to the action they eventually took, demonstrating their faith in God and His Word. Each situation had an "impossible" attached to it that challenged them. Today, will you ask God to open your eyes to understand the challenges, and help you step out in faith, leaning wholly on your Lord?

READ AND STUDY GOD'S WORD

1. Today you are going to walk again through God's Gallery of Faith, looking at each person carefully to recognize the one thing that made their situation seem difficult and maybe even impossible, thus testing their faith in God and His Word. Read Hebrews 11 and write out all

that you see about the things that can test our faith. You may use a Journal page if you need more space. For example, in Hebrews 11:8 we see that Abraham didn't know where he was going. God bless you as you live in His Word today.

2. What is the most important truth you learned in your study today?

ADORE GOD IN PRAYER

Talk with God about what you have learned today. Turn to your Prayer pages and write out all the requests you have for your Lord. Ask Him to help you step out in faith, holding on to His promises.

YIELD YOURSELF TO GOD

See how much God thinks of faith. It is priceless in His esteem. What gold is to the miser, faith is to God. It is the root of all other grace, the germ of the saintly life, the key to the divine storehouse, the foot of the heavenly ladder, the earthward pier of the arch that bridges the abyss between the unseen and the seen. To make it strong in one poor heart is a matter of extreme value in His sight. And since it can only grow strong by use, and exercise, and strain, be not surprised if He exposes you to discipline, graduated according to your power, but becoming ever severer, until beneath His gracious tuition the faith which once shivered at sight of the shallows will plunge fearlessly into the deep, and do business in mighty waters.[10]

F.B. MEYER in TRIED BY FIRE

ENJOY HIS PRESENCE

Today you can know that you are not alone in your times of fear and discouragement. All the great men and women of God have also experienced fiery trials. And yet, they emerged victorious and triumphant. And you can, too. Learn these secrets of faith. Find and live in God's promises, His say-so's, and you will discover renewed strength to realize the unseen realities of God and His Word always have priority and rule and reign. God has said it and that settles it. And you have the strength and power of Christ Himself to live by faith, taking God at His Word. How has this study helped you recognize the ways your faith is being tested and what promises do you need to hold on to today?

REST IN HIS LOVE

"They were stoned, they were sawn in two, they were tempted, they were put to death with the sword; they went about in sheepskins, in goatskins, being destitute, afflicted, ill-treated (men of whom the world was not worthy)…" (Hebrews 11:37-38).

THE ETERNAL WORD

The grass withers, the flower fades, but the word of our God stands forever. Isaiah 40:8
Zion National Park, Utah, USA
Nikon D7000, ISO 160, f11.0, 3 Bracketed EXP, Adobe Photoshop, Nik Silver Efex Pro
MYPHOTOWALK.COM—CATHERINEMARTIN.SMUGMUG.COM

DISCOVERING THE PROMISES OF FAITH

He was looking for the city which has foundations, whose architect and builder is God.

HEBREWS 11:10

PREPARE YOUR HEART

A Dutch fairy tale describes a woman who built her entire life on greed and money. She was the most well known person in her town. The tale goes on to describe how everything she was investing in was lost or destroyed. Ultimately, her entire town was flooded and sank under the water. The story ends this way: "Even to this day, when the water is calm and clear, fishermen sailing from the modern town that bears the ancient city's name can see the towers and steeples… sometimes fish swimming through the belfries cause the bells to toll. Then a sound of faraway tinkling can be heard floating above the watery depths…a warning to all who hear it of the punishment of greed."[11]

Jesus taught that there are two ways a person can build their lives—wisely building on rock by acting on what He says or foolishly building on sand by not acting on what He says. Jesus continued His lesson in Matthew 7:24-27 by demonstrating that if we are wise, building our lives on what He says, then when the rain and floods and strong winds beat against our house, it will not fall because it is founded on a rock.

In our last day of study this week, we are going to focus on building our lives on God's promises and the magnificent results of such a life. We have been living in Hebrews 11 and have filled our hearts and minds with many examples of those who wisely chose to live by faith. We also want to be heroes of the faith, making wise choices, day by day, to invest in God and His promises. Ask God now to speak to your heart as you draw near to Him today.

READ AND STUDY GOD'S WORD

1. You have been living in God's Gallery of Faith, and now, you are going to walk through its hallways one more time. As you read Hebrews 11, look for the promises of God each person counted on, and the amazing results of their faith. These are the promises that enabled each person to walk on water with their faith. For example Abraham believed the promise of heaven and a city prepared there by God. The amazing result of his faith is that he left his secure home and went to the promised land. Another example is Sarah who believed God's promise that she would have a child even though she was too old for childbearing. The result is that she bore a son, and out of that lineage came Jesus, the Messiah. You may use a Journal page if you need more space in your study today.

2. What is the most important truth you have learned from your study in Hebrews 11 today?

ADORE GOD IN PRAYER

Lord
When I feel I can't possibly make it
When I feel deluged with problems
When I feel helpless
Against the strange twistings of life
When I feel there is no way out
The FACT is
You have a Plan
You know what You're about.
The FACT is
The greater the strategy of the Enemy
The greater the assurance of victory.
The FACT is
The worst may seem to happen
But the best is on the way.
God, hold me to the facts.[12]

RUTH HARMS CALKIN IN I KEEP RUNNING BACK TO YOU

YIELD YOURSELF TO GOD

Is Christ yours? Then His promises are yours.

ANDREW BONAR

Thank God, none of these promises are out of date, or grown stale. They are as fresh and vigorous and young and sweet as ever.

D.L. MOODY

What are the results of living by God's promises? How about overcoming obstacles in your life? How about enjoying a deeper relationship with God? Or how about reaping a glorious destiny? God has designed each of us uniquely, and His promises will be fulfilled in your life by faith, in accordance with His faithfulness and His desired end for you.[13]

NICK HARRISON IN POWER IN THE PROMISES

ENJOY HIS PRESENCE

Dear friend, what a week of study in Hebrews 11 this week. You have invested valuable time studying God's Word and it will reap eternal results. Think about all you have learned. What is the most significant insight and lesson you will take with you from this week? What is your favorite promise? Close by writing a prayer in your Journal expressing all that is on your heart.

REST IN HIS LOVE

"…she considered Him faithful who had promised." (Hebrews 11:11).

THE MAGNIFICENT PROMISES OF GOD

He has granted to us His precious and magnificent promises. 2 Peter 1:4
Zion National Park, Utah, USA
Nikon D7000, ISO 160, f14.0, 3 Bracketed EXP, Adobe Photoshop, Nik Silver Efex Pro
MYPHOTOWALK.COM—CATHERINEMARTIN.SMUGMUG.COM

DEVOTIONAL READING
BY ANNIE JOHNSON FLINT

DEAR FRIEND,

The next two days are your opportunity to review what you have learned this week. Thank the Lord for all He is teaching you about faith. As you think about how to have walk on water faith in light of Hebrews 11, record your:

Most meaningful insight:

Most meaningful devotional reading:

Most meaningful verse:

Your most significant promise this week written in A Promise A Day:

Linger long in these words by Annie Johnson Flint, one who suffered the effects of crippling arthritis, yet discovered the strength of God and His promises.

I would not lose the hard things from my life,
The rocks o'er which I stumbled long ago,
The grief and fears, the failures and mistakes,
That tried and tested faith and patience so.

I need them now; they make the deep-laid wall,
The firm foundation-stones on which I raise—
To mount therein from stair to higher stair—
The lofty towers of my House of Praise.
Soft was the roadside turf to weary feet,
And cool the meadows where I fain had trod,
And sweet beneath the trees to lie at rest
And breathe the incense of the flower-starred sod;
But not on these might I securely build,
Nor sand nor sod withstand the earthquake shock.
I need the rough, hard boulders of the hills
To set my house on everlasting rock.[14]

ANNIE JOHNSON FLINT IN BEST-LOVED POEMS

In summary, 11:1-40 leads the audience into God's Hall of Fame. Here they listen to the roll-call of approved models of committed faithfulness who clarify for us the role of faith in the life of the man or woman of God. They acted in their present in the light of the certainty of the promised future.[15]

WILLIAM LANE IN HEBREWS, A CALL TO COMMITMENT

Think through these encouraging words from D. Martyn Lloyd Jones about faith: God is the ruler of the universe, and we are known to Him one by one, and are in a personal relationship to Him. It was the faith of all the great heroes of the faith described in Hebrews 11. That is what kept those men going. Quite frequently they did not understand but they said, "God knows and God undertakes." They had this final confidence that He who had brought them into being, and who had a purpose for them, would not leave them or forsake them. He would surely sustain and lead them all the journey through, until their purpose in this world had been completed, and He would receive them into their heavenly habitation where they would spend their eternity in His glorious presence…Argue it out, start with first principles and draw the inevitable deduction. The moment you do so, care and worry and anxiety will vanish, and as a child of your heavenly Father you will walk with peace and serenity in the direction of your everlasting home. [16]

Viewer Guide
❧ WEEK THREE ❧

Faith That Leaves A Legacy

This week we studied an overview of Hebrews 11, God's Gallery of Faith. And today in our time together, we are going to see the power of having great examples in heroes of the faith. I want your life to be a legacy of faith, the kind of faith that others can imitate. So grab your Bible, and let's get into the Word of God together.

"Remember those who led you, who spoke the word of God to you; and considering the result of their conduct, imitate their faith" (Hebrews 13:7).

Every day, every moment, our lives are _____, and leaving behind us a _____. Our lives are leaving a _____. People will be _____ and have a memory of that message.

God's encouragements for us from Hebrews 13:7:

1. _____those who led you.

Remember means "to be mindful of" and "to keep in mind."

Pay _____ to your leaders.

2. Consider the _____ of their conduct.

Consider means "to look back upon, scan closely, observe attentively, and look back carefully on."

Our faith has a great and awesome _____.

3. _____ their faith.

Imitate means to "emulate" and carries the idea of mimicking in a positive way.

The faith-walking person takes God at His _____.

Who are those who have led you, who have a faith that can be imitated?

Do you have a faith that can be imitated?

❧ *Video messages are available on DVDs or as Digital M4V Video. Audio messages are available as Digital MP3 Audio. Visit the Quiet Time Ministries Online Store at www.quiettime.org.*

THE FAITH OF ABRAHAM, THE FRIEND OF GOD

Hebrews 11:8-19, Romans 4

Faith is only the link of union, but inasmuch as it unites us to the Son of God, it brings us into the enjoyment of all that He is as the Alpha and Omega, the Beginning and the End, the First and the Last.[1]

F.B. MEYER

WHEN YOU HEAR GOD SPEAK

After this, the word of the LORD came to Abram in a vision; "Do not be afraid, Abram. I am your shield, your very great reward."

GENESIS 15:1 NIV

PREPARE YOUR HEART

Martin Luther was walking down a road one day and suddenly a thunderstorm moved into the area. He was struck by lightning and knocked to the ground. Through that experience Martin Luther became convinced he should become a monk, and he joined the monastery at Erfurt in 1505 at the age of 21. Life in the monastery was rigorous, beginning with prayer between 1 and 2 AM. Luther's days were filled with ritual, ceremony, sacraments, and penance. The truth is that Martin Luther was in search of peace with God. He wanted to become a friend of God, accepted, and made right with God. So he worked for years trying to achieve righteousness, and attempting to gain acceptance from God. He was obsessed with confessing all known sin, yet he experienced deep feelings of guilt and despair. He was especially frustrated by the words of Romans 1:17, "the righteous man shall live by faith." These words seemed to imply to him that he would always experience punishment by God because he could never measure up to God's righteousness. He tried a new way to get the forgiveness and acceptance he wanted so much. He thought going to Rome, where the Pope was, and where the priests and cardinals served, would be the answer. So in 1510-1511 he traveled to Rome. What he discovered there shocked and disgusted him. He witnessed immorality among the religious leaders, scandalous behavior, and arrogant attitudes. The things he heard and saw disillusioned him, so he sought a new way to reach God. Outside a building called the Lateran, there were some ancient stairs from Jerusalem thought to have been walked on by Jesus Himself. The belief was that if you crawled on hands and knees up those stairs praying, step by step, you would make a special impression on God. Martin Luther crawled up those stairs, one by one. When he reached the top, he looked back down, and was struck with the ridiculous nature of what he had just done, thinking "What if this is not true?" He went back to Germany, deeply troubled. The turning point came when he was studying the book of Romans in preparation to teach a Bible class. He read Romans 1:16-17 again, a passage he had lived in many times before. But this time, a light flooded his very mind, heart, and soul and he realized the truth of the words, "But the righteous man shall live by faith." God spoke to him, and showed him that righteousness comes only by faith. No work of his could ever bring about the righteousness of God. Thus began his own personal life reformation, and that was the beginning of what has been known as the Reformation, the dawn of a new day and a new understanding of salvation by grace through faith.

There comes a day when you hear God speak in His Word. And when you hear Him speak, you are changed forever. He truly does transform you by changing the way you think. And that is the power that comes from the promises in His Word.

We have been studying what it means to have a walk on water faith. It's the faith that defies adverse circumstances and enables you to walk through difficulties, empowered by God. We have looked at the example of Peter, who literally got out of the boat and walked on water when Jesus said, "Come." We learned about the school of faith, where Jesus is our teacher, the author and perfecter of our faith, and we experience the tests of faith and spiritual growth in our faith. Then, we walked through God's Gallery of Faith, looking at one example after another of those who have gone before us, grasping God's promise, His say-so, and living by faith. And now, we are going to look more closely at the lives of some of those great heroes of the faith in Hebrews 11, beginning with Abraham, who was called the Friend of God by God Himself (Isaiah 41:8) and the man of faith (Galatians 3:9 ESV). Your goal this week is to grow deeper in your own faith walk through lessons learned from the life of Abraham.

Now, as you draw near to God, begin your quiet time by writing a prayer expressing all that is on your heart.

READ AND STUDY GOD'S WORD

1. In Week 3 we learned that Hebrews 11 is an important part of a sermon written to encourage believers who are suffering and have lost confidence. Hebrews is a call to a new commitment and Hebrews 11 demonstrates that commitment by looking at heroes of the faith. And one of the most important heroes is Abraham. God called Abraham "My friend" in Isaiah 41:8. And how did this relationship with God begin? God spoke to Abraham. Read the following verses and record what you learn about the words spoken to Abraham.

Genesis 12:1-5

Genesis 15:1-5

Genesis 17:1-8

2. In Genesis 12, 15 and 17, God has given Abraham some very powerful promises. These promises are the "I Am's" and the "I Will's" of God, where He tells us who He is and what He does. In fact, Galatians 3:18 confirms that God in His grace was giving Abraham a promise. Faith responds to the promises of God with a resolve and action based on truth from God's Word. Read the following verses to begin discovering why Abraham is considered a hero in God's Gallery of Faith in Hebrews 11. Write out Abraham's responses and actions of faith.

Genesis 15:6

Romans 4:1-3

Romans 4:13

Hebrews 11:8-10

3. What is the most important truth you have learned today?

ADORE GOD IN PRAYER

Pray the words of F.B. Meyer today: "Open to me, O Spirit of Truth, the treasures of your holy Word, that my soul may be continually enriched, and that I may abound in every good word and work."[2]

YIELD YOURSELF TO GOD

If there is a desire in your heart for more of God's blessing in your life, turn your attention to the details of Abraham's encounters with God. You will find yourself back at the center, at the beating heart of living religion…Abraham had only his own empty, hungry heart. That and the manifestation of the God who reveals Himself to men and women who desire to find Him and know Him! The Bible informs us that Abraham heard the word of the Lord…The Lord God was about to do something special in our sinful world. He needed a man who would believe and trust and obey just because God is God! Abraham was that man…Abraham had a glorious and continuing experience with the Almighty God.…Think about the reality of Abraham's experience. Abraham was consciously aware of God, His presence and His revelation. He was aware that the living God had stepped over the threshold into personal encounter with a man who found the desire within himself to know God, to believe God and to live for God…Abraham was lying face down in humility and reverence, overcome with awe in this encounter with God. He knew that he was surrounded by the world's greatest mystery. The presence of this One who fills all things was pressing in upon him, rising above him, defeating him, taking away his natural self-confidence. God was overwhelming him and yet inviting and calling him, pleading with him and promising him a great future as a friend of God! This is God's way and God's plan. This is God…Do not miss the application of truth here. God was saying to Abraham, "You may have some other idea about the design and purpose for your life, but you are wrong! You were created in My image to worship Me and to glorify Me…commit your whole life and future into My hands. Let Me as your Creator and God fulfill in you My perfect design. It is My great desire that you become a faithful and delighted worshiper at My throne."[3]

A.W. TOZER IN MEN WHO MET GOD

ENJOY HIS PRESENCE

Abraham heard God speak and responded to the "I Am" and "I Will" promises from God. God wants you to hear Him speak in His Word. He says in Isaiah 40:28 "Do you not know? Have you not heard?" What will it take for you to hear God speak His "I Am's" of who He is and the "I Will's" of what He does to you? Hear it from God Himself: "Be still and know that I am God" (Psalm 46:10 NIV). You need quiet time where you can be still and open the pages of His Word to hear Him speak. Will you resolve to slow down and draw near to God in quiet and solitude? Will you hold His Word closer to your heart? Close your time now by writing a prayer to the Lord asking Him to give you a new and deeper love for Him and His Word. Ask Him for His promise for you today. And ask Him to give you eyes to see and ears to hear all that He has to say to you.

REST IN HIS LOVE

"By faith Abraham, when he was called, obeyed…" (Hebrews 11:8).

SOUL REVIVAL

The instructions of the LORD are perfect, reviving the soul. Psalm 19:7 NLT
Zion National Park, Utah, USA
Nikon D7000, ISO 160, f22.0, 1/15, Adobe Photoshop, Nik Silver Efex Pro
MYPHOTOWALK.COM—CATHERINEMARTIN.SMUGMUG.COM

WHEN YOU DON'T KNOW

By faith Abraham, when he was called, obeyed by going out to a place which he was to receive for an inheritance; and he went out, not knowing where he was going.

HEBREWS 11:8

PREPARE YOUR HEART

Have you ever experienced a time when you didn't understand how the circumstances of your life could possibly be part of God's plan? You have served the Lord, loved Him, walked in His ways, but your life took an unexpected turn, and you feel lost. You have no idea where you are going. And yet, you have heard God speak. You know and love Him. But you can't see the destination. Learn the lesson of Abraham. He was in just such a circumstance. And he is a hero of the faith. Heroes of faith experience unexplained turns in their lives. Sometimes their walk of faith is surrounded with fog, yet they have God's Word as a lamp for their feet and a light for their path (Psalm 119:105). Today, as you spend time with God in His Word, ask Him to speak to you from the example of Abraham, the friend of God.

READ AND STUDY GOD'S WORD

1. Abraham heard God speak and responded to God's promises with a great action of faith. Read Hebrews 11:8-9 and record Abraham's actions of faith and the challenges to his life in stepping out in faith.

2. Abraham received God's promises and heard God explain that He was Abraham's shield and great reward (Genesis 15:1) and that He was El Shaddai (Almighty God Genesis 17:1). He promised His presence in Abraham's life and a covenant relationship (Genesis 17:1-3). Abraham took these promises into account and responded in faith. Read Hebrews 11:10 and 13-16 and write about the perspective of Abraham based on God's promises.

3. Read Romans 4:3-5 and Romans 4:18 and write what you learn about Abraham's faith.

4. Abraham had a "hope against hope" belief (Romans 4:18). This means "he continued to believe in God even when all grounds for human hope were gone."[4] What do you think was Abraham's greatest encouragement for this kind of faith that enabled him to follow the Lord though he did not know where he was going?

ADORE GOD IN PRAYER

David, the man after God's own heart, discovered that "those who know Your name will put their trust in You" (Psalm 9:10). Those who have the greatest trust and faith, know God best. Because they know Him, they trust Him. They trust even though they do not understand (Proverbs 3:5). They have listened to God say Who He is in His Word, and have responded with a faith-filled "Yes, Lord." Today, as you talk with God, turn to Psalm 46, note all you learn about God, and personalize the words in prayer to Him.

YIELD YOURSELF TO GOD

Abraham is mentioned as an example of faith because he lived his days on this earth in faith that God would guide him through the circumstances of life and lead him to the heavenly city. Abraham's life is, therefore, strangely similar to ours as Christians—sojourners in places which are not our real homes...By faith, we live as foreigners in a strange land, looking for the celestial city. While in this strange land, we must trust the Lord to guide us through our struggles, difficulties, sufferings, and unexpected turns. The reason we can do so is because we know that God uses them all to display the gospel of Jesus through our enduring faith.[5]

BRIAN CROFT IN A FAITH THAT ENDURES

We can learn much from Abraham for our own walk of faith. He felt that the will of God was right and the summons clear; he was wise enough to obey at once. Though he did not know where he was being led, he was certain that God knew. Love would not give less than its best. He was certain that God never mocked those who fixed their trust in Him. Faith became his sole authority, his sufficient warrant; he was ready for any risk or loss obedience might demand. He willingly waived his present security for an unknown future, leaving his rightful inheritance for a greater one yet to come. Abraham had only God's promise, but his faith regarded all God's promises as equal to His performances. From that day when Abraham left Ur, his faith and love precluded any provider or protector but God alone. He gave himself entirely to the One who promised, "Fear not, Abram, I am your shield; your reward shall be very great" (Genesis 15:1). Although dispossessed of his earthly security, God's friend became the true heir of heaven's riches and relationships.[6]

DWIGHT HERVEY SMALL IN NO RIVAL LOVE

ENJOY HIS PRESENCE

As you think about all you've learned from the life of Abraham today, where are you? Is there something in your life that you are relying on as an earthly security instead of relying and trusting in the Lord? Is there a promise from the Lord that has given you incredible hope, prompting a deeper faith. Write your thoughts and a prayer in response to what God is teaching you.

REST IN HIS LOVE

"God is our refuge and strength, a very present help in trouble. Therefore we will not fear, though the earth should change and though the mountains slip into the heart of the sea; though its waters roar and foam, though the mountains quake at its swelling pride. There is a river whose streams make glad the city of God, the holy dwelling places of the Most High. God is in the midst of her, she will not be moved; God will help her when the morning dawns" (Psalm 46:1-5).

GOD IS MY HOPE

My soul, wait in silence for God only, for my hope is from Him. Psalm 62:5
Zion National Park, Utah, USA
Nikon D7000, ISO 125, f4.5, 1/1000, Adobe Photoshop, Nik Silver Efex Pro
MYPHOTOWALK.COM—CATHERINEMARTIN.SMUGMUG.COM

WHEN YOU WALK WITH GOD

God told him, "I have made you the father of many nations." This happened because Abraham believed in the God who brings the dead back to life and who creates new things out of nothing..

ROMANS 4:17 NLT

PREPARE YOUR HEART

A.W. Tozer was invited to speak in McAllen, Texas. He got an idea to write a book on the long train ride. He asked for a small writing table and began to write. He kept writing all night long and at 7:30 AM the next morning, the book was finished. And that is the story of how Tozer wrote the bestselling, beloved *The Pursuit of God*. What is the secret of a life who can write books with such depth and purpose? Tozer had found a quiet place apart from the world where he spent hours in prayer, with only his Bible and hymnal as companions. Lyle Dorsett, in his biography *A Passion For God*, wrote: "Spiritually alert Christians said that the 'bouquet of the Holy Spirit' was all over A.W. Tozer. Others used different rhetoric, saying that he had the 'sacred anointing' or that it was evident 'he had been with Jesus.' Tozer never denied that he spent many hours in prayer out of his increasingly demanding schedule. On the contrary, he maintained that anyone who wanted to know Christ better and love Him more must devote time to closet prayer."[7]

Would you like to become someone who knows God and walks with Him in life? Today, you are going to learn more about this kind of life from our hero of the faith, Abraham. Abraham was one who lived and walked in the presence of God. And you can do the same. Walking with God is a secret to having a walk on water faith.

READ AND STUDY GOD'S WORD

1. In Romans 4:17 we learn that Abraham was in the presence of God. He had contact with God. And in Isaiah 41:8 God called Abraham His friend. How did such a friendship occur? Abraham spent time with God and talked with Him. Read the following passages of Scripture and write out what you notice about Abraham's relationship with God.

Genesis 12:7-8, 13:4

Genesis 17:1-3

Genesis 18:1-33

Genesis 21:1-2

Genesis 21:33

2. In Genesis 17:1-3 God made a covenant with Abraham, a most solemn, binding agreement. This covenant held the promise of land and descendants, and also a relationship with God as Abraham walked before the Lord and was blameless. The relationship was based on covenant. And your relationship with God also has a covenant as its foundation—the new covenant ratified in the blood of Christ Himself. In Jeremiah 31:31-34 God speaks of this new covenant where He will put the law within and write it on our hearts. Hebrews 8:6 shows the power of this new covenant, "He is also the mediator of a better covenant, which has been enacted on better promises." Dear friend, you need to know that God desires a relationship with you. He is calling you to Himself. "For God so loved the world, that He gave His only begotten Son, that whoever believes in Him shall not perish, but have eternal life" (John 3:16). Think about those words, "eternal life." The Lord wants you to be with Him forever. In John 14:3 Jesus explains He is preparing a place for us and that He will come again and receive us to Himself, "that where I am, you may be also." Oh, those are wonderful words to hear today! He wants us with Him always. And not only did He call Abraham a friend, but He also calls us His friends. He says, "I have called you friends, for all things that I have heard from My Father I have made known to you" (John 15:15). You are invited into the inner circle of friendship with the Lord Jesus Christ.

Will you commit to an intimate relationship with the Lord? Will you spend quiet time with Him everyday and draw near to Him in His Word? Think about all you are learning about your relationship with God. How does Abraham's relationship with God encourage you in your relationship with the Lord? And how does faith—taking God at His Word—help you in walking intimately, moment by moment, with the Lord each day? And how does an intimate relationship with the Lord help grow your faith? What promises do you need to consider and hold dear today to walk with intimately with your Lord?

ADORE GOD IN PRAYER

> "Lord, I would trust Thee completely; I would be altogether Thine; I would exalt Thee above all. I desire that I may feel no sense of possessing anything outside of Thee. I want constantly to be aware of Thine overshadowing Presence and to hear Thy speaking Voice. I long to live in restful sincerity of heart. I want to live so fully in the Spirit that all my thought may be as sweet incense ascending to Thee and every act of my life may be an act of worship. Therefore I pray in the words of Thy great servant of old, 'I beseech Thee so for to cleanse the intent of mine heart with the unspeakable gift of Thy grace, that I may perfectly love Thee and worthily praise Thee.' And all this I confidently believe Thou wilt grant me through the merits of Jesus Christ Thy Son. Amen."[8]

A.W. TOZER IN THE PURSUIT OF GOD

YIELD YOURSELF TO GOD

Meditate on the following words by A.W. Tozer:

> What higher privilege and experience is granted to mankind on earth than to be admitted into the circles of the friends of God? Abraham, called in the Bible the father of the faithful, demonstrated in many ways that he had experienced the reality of another and better world. He saw that sphere, that kingdom in which a

living God reigns and rules and still encourages men and women to become His friends—It is well for us to remember that Divine-human friendship originated with God. Had God not first said, "You are My friends," it would be inexcusably brash for any man to say, "I am a friend of God." But since God claims us for His friends, it is an act of unbelief to deny the offer of such a relationship…Genuine Christian experience must always include an encounter with God Himself. The spiritual giants of old were those who at some time became acutely conscious of the presence of God. They maintained that consciousness for the rest of their lives…The essential point is this: These were men who met and experienced God… they had become friends of God…they walked in conscious communion with the real Presence and addressed their prayers to God with the artless conviction that they were truly addressing Someone actually there… [9]

A.W. TOZER IN MEN WHO MET GOD

ENJOY HIS PRESENCE

In Abraham we have a man of God who walked intimately with God. Consciously aware of His presence, he talked with the Lord. They were friends. Are you a friend of God? Close by writing a prayer expressing all that is on your heart. And ask the Lord, the One who loves you, for His promise today, then write it out in A Promise A Day.

REST IN HIS LOVE

"I have called you friends, for all things that I have heard from My Father I have made known to you" (John 15:15).

KNOWING THE LORD

Let us press on to know the LORD. His going forth is as certain as the dawn. Hosea 6:3
Zion National Park, Utah, USA
Nikon D7000, ISO 160, f22.0, 1.3, Adobe Photoshop, Nik Silver Efex Pro
MYPHOTOWALK.COM—CATHERINEMARTIN.SMUGMUG.COM

WHEN YOU SURRENDER YOUR DREAM

*With respect to the promise of God, he did not waver in unbelief but
grew strong in faith, giving glory to God, and being fully assured
that what God had promised, He was able also to perform.*

ROMANS 4:20-21

PREPARE YOUR HEART

Lilias Trotter was born in the 1800's in England as the daughter of a distinguished Victorian family. She was brilliantly gifted as an artist and was heralded by John Ruskin, a well-known artist of the day as someone who could become one of the nation's finest artists. She also loved Christ and grew in her faith under the teaching of such well-known Christians as Robert Pearsall Smith and D.L. Moody. Ruskin took Lilias and her mother throughout Venice, showing them paintings and sculpture he thought would train Lilias' artistic eye. Under his tutelage, Lilias developed in her artistic ability, especially in watercolors. She would often send Ruskin paintings for him to critique. At the same time, Lilias was involved in ministry, and loved her work at Welbeck Street Institute. The demands of ministry increased with time to the point where Ruskin challenged Lilias to decide between her art and ministry for the Lord. He set before her an opportunity to learn from him where she would have a brilliant future if she would devote herself wholeheartedly to her art. She experienced a great crisis of heart. In a letter written to a friend at that time requesting prayer to clearly see God's plan, she wrote that Ruskin had told her "she would be the greatest living painter and do things Immortal."[10] She was only twenty-six years old, yet brought to a place of deep surrender to the Lord and His ways. In the end, Lilias turned down Ruskin's offer, choosing to give herself in utter abandonment to follow the Lord and His will for her life. It came down to a decision that she could not give herself to art in the way Ruskin desired, but only in the way that God wanted for her. And in fact, the surrender of that dream envisioned in her mind one way developed into a dream of another kind. The Lord called her as a missionary in Algiers ten years later where she lived among the Arab people of Algeria. Her artwork filled her journals and two books she wrote, *Parables of the Cross* and *Parables of the Christ Life*. In addition, God gave her a wonderful friend during her lifetime, who corresponded with her, and encouraged her—the great faith hero, Amy Carmichael.

Have you ever sensed that God is asking you to surrender a dream? You need to know whatever you lay down will not be without fruit. God has a way of taking all our surrenders and multiplying them into something new and more bountiful. Today, as you spend time with the Lord, ask Him to speak to you from the life and faith of Abraham.

READ AND STUDY GOD'S WORD

1. Abraham was given the promise that he would be the father of a great nation and have an infinite number of descendents. God's promise was seemingly impossible because his wife, Sarah, was unable to have any children. Sarah grew impatient and gave Abraham her Egyptian maid to bear a child. Genesis 16:2 says that "Abram listened to the voice of Sarai" and so Hagar also became his wife, and bore him a child. God came to Abraham again and confirmed His promise to Abraham in Genesis 17:1-17. Abraham responded with laughter and asked if Ishmael was the answer to God's promise. God replied, "No, but Sarah your wife will bear you a son, and you shall call his name Isaac, and I will establish My covenant with him for an everlasting covenant for his descendants after him" (Genesis 17:19). Now, we will see the fulfillment of that promise. Read Genesis 21:1-3 and write out how God fulfilled His promise to Abraham.

2. Read Romans 4:18-21 and write out how Abraham dealt with his impossibilities and God's promises in the birth of Isaac. What held more importance and focus for Abraham—the impossibilities or God's promise? We know that Abraham grew strong in faith in God's promises. The Greek word for "grew strong" in Romans 4:20 is *endunamoo* in the Greek and means to be strengthened, equipped, enabled, made capable, and strengthened in soul and purpose. How does this help you understand faith and the power of the promises of God? Think through the surrender that is necessary in the face of an impossibility.

3. And now comes the great test, proving the faith of Abraham. Read about it in Genesis 22:1-14 and James 2:20-23. What did Abraham need to surrender and what actions do you see as demonstrations of his faith in God? How did his surrender relate to and impact his faith?

4. Hebrews 11:17-19 offers insight into how Abraham reasoned through God's request and what helped him in his great moment of faith. Read Hebrews 11:17-19 and write out what you learn.

5. In 2 Peter 1:4 we see that God "has granted to us His precious and magnificent promises, so that by them you may become partakers of the divine nature, having escaped the corruption that is in the world by lust." How does Abraham's example help you understand the greatness of God's promises, learn how to reason through God's promises, and grow strong in faith in light of your own impossible circumstances?

ADORE GOD IN PRAYER

Turn to your Prayer pages and use one of the pages for all that is on your heart today that needs to be surrendered to Him. What promises can you hold on to in your surrenders following your example, Abraham? Record all the requests that are on your heart, one by one in the spaces provided. Then, watch eagerly in the days to come as God responds to your prayers.

YIELD YOURSELF TO GOD

By faith you can extract the comfort of a promise from most scriptures. There are innumerable types and implied promises that we can apply. A life of faith lives in the strength of a promise. Faith reasons with God on the basis of His promises with a holy kind of reasoning…If you bring faith to a promise you bring that which is most pleasing to God. And claiming one promise gives you an interest in all. The first act of faith gives you an interest in Christ, and all who have Christ, have all. He that believes has a right to all the promises, and may confidently apply them all. God had you in mind when He made the promise. What a sweet encouragement is this! Act and live by faith, and consider that you were in the thoughts and eyes of God when He promised.[11]

DAVID CLARKSON IN VOICES FROM THE PAST

Take the very hardest thing in your life—the place of difficulty, outward or inward, and expect God to triumph gloriously in that very spot. Just there He can bring your soul into blossom.

LILIAS TROTTER IN PARABLES OF THE CROSS

Beloved, this must ever be a typical scene in every transformed life. There comes a crisis-hour to each of us, if God has called us to the highest and best, when all resources fail; when we face either ruin or something higher than we ever dreamed; when we must have infinite help from God and yet, ere ye can have it, we must let something go; we must surrender completely; we must cease from our own wisdom, strength, and righteousness, and become crucified with Christ and alive in Him. God knows how to lead us up to this crisis, and He knows how to lead us through.

MRS. CHARLES COWMAN IN STREAMS IN THE DESERT

Oh for a faith like this! To simply believe what God says; to be assured that God will do just what He has promised; looking without alarm, from circumstances that threaten to make the fulfillment impossible, to the bare word of God's unswerving truthfulness.[12]

F.B. Meyer in Great Men Of The Bible

Enjoy His Presence

Abraham teaches us how to have a walk on water faith. Remember, faith is the ability to see beyond temporal circumstances to the eternal realities of God and His promises, and as a result, takes God at His Word and acts on His promises in spite of conflicting circumstances, thoughts, and feelings. At times, your circumstances, thoughts, and feelings can call into question what God has promised you in His Word about Himself and all that He can do in your life. In Abraham's case, he saw his own temporal circumstance but moved past it to God's promise and grew strong in faith and gave glory to God. And he obeyed God in spite of his own dreams and desires.

Perhaps in your case you have not had the choice. A dream you had was seemingly taken from you. And perhaps you are filled with such disappointment that you have taken a few steps backward. Will you let go of the one thing today, in order to receive back from the Lord what His grace has ready for you? Will you remember who God is and all He promises for you even in the midst of loss? Therein is the need for surrender. Don't waste another minute. Remember the truth that "God is able to make all grace abound to you, so that always having all sufficiency in everything, you may have an abundance for every good deed" (2 Corinthians 9:8). By His grace He will flood you with His power and faith for every storm. You can know that "The Lord God is a sun and shield; The Lord gives grace and glory; no good thing does He withhold from those who walk uprightly" (Psalm 84:11).

How can you look to Jesus, listen to Jesus, respond to Jesus, believe Jesus, pray to Jesus, and worship Jesus today? What is His promise for you? What is your response to the Lord? God bless you today, dear friend.

REST IN HIS LOVE

"God is able to make all grace abound to you, so that always having all sufficiency in everything, you may have an abundance for every good deed" (2 Corinthians 9:8).

TRANSFORMATION

Let God transform you into a new person by changing the way you think. Romans 12:2
Zion National Park, Utah, USA

Nikon D7000, ISO 160, f11.0, 3 Bracketed EXP, Adobe Photoshop, Nik Silver Efex Pro
MYPHOTOWALK.COM—CATHERINEMARTIN.SMUGMUG.COM

WHEN YOU RECEIVE FAITH'S REWARD

For this, O LORD, I will praise you among the nations; I will sing praises to your name.
Psalm 18:49 nlt

PREPARE YOUR HEART

Faith never goes unnoticed in heaven and reaps a rich reward. Hebrews 11 is filled with amazing results of faith. We see in Hebrews 11:33 that kingdoms were conquered, acts of righteousness were performed, promises were obtained, mouths of lions were shut, the power of fire was quenched, the edge of the sword was escaped, the weak were made strong, might was experienced in war, and foreign armies were put to flight. Seeing God at work is a great blessing. There is nothing so exciting as watching Him change lives. Today you are going to have the opportunity to see the results and reward of Abraham's faith.

READ AND STUDY GOD'S WORD

1. What a blessing to look at the faith of Abraham this week. Just think about the kind of faith that pleases God and makes a man His friend. That's the kind of faith we want to have. To please God and be His friend is great reward in itself and enough blessing to last a lifetime. There were even more results and reward for Abraham's faith. Look at the following verses and write out what you learn.

Genesis 24:1

Isaiah 41:8

Isaiah 51:2

Matthew 1:1

Romans 4:3

Romans 4:16

Galatians 3:6-9

Hebrews 6:13-15

Hebrews 11:11

James 2:23

2. Abraham believed God—he had faith in God—and it was credited to him as "righteousness" (Romans 4:3). The Greek word for righteousness is *dikaiosune* and means God's uprightness and right standard. What happened is that Abraham was credited with right standing with God as a gift of grace. Righteousness was faith's wonderful reward. We learn through Abraham and throughout the Bible that no one can earn righteousness. Jesus died on the cross so that we might become righteous in Him (2 Corinthians 5:21). This righteousness is offered to all of us if we will receive Christ "by grace through faith" (Ephesians 2:8-9). Read Galatians 3:23-29 and record what you learn about your own faith and the great reward you have as a result.

ADORE GOD IN PRAYER

Talk with God today thanking Him for all He has taught you through the life of Abraham. Ask Him to give you the kind of walk on water faith that Abraham lived out in his lifetime.

YIELD YOURSELF TO GOD

And can it be that I should gain an interest in the Savior's blood?
Died He for me who caused His pain? For me, who Him to death pursued?
Amazing love! how can it be that Thou, my God should die for me?
Amazing love! how can it be that Thou, my God, shouldst die for me!

He left His Father's throne above, so free, so infinite His grace!
Emptied Himself of all but love, and bled for Adam's helpless race!
'Tis mercy all, immense and free, For, O my God, it found out me.
Amazing love! how can it be that Thou, my God, shouldst die for me!

Long my imprisoned spirit lay fastbound in sin and nature's night.
Thine eye diffused a quickening ray; I woke, the dungeon flamed with light!
My chains fell off, my heart was free, I rose, went forth, and followed Thee.
Amazing love! how can it be that Thou, my God, shouldst die for me!

No condemnation now I dread: Jesus, and all in Him, is mine!
Alive in Him, my living Head, and clothed in righteousness divine.
Bold I approach th'eternal throne, and claim the crown, through Christ my own.
Amazing love! how can it be that Thou, my God, shouldst die for me!

CHARLES WESLEY

ENJOY HIS PRESENCE

Oh those words of Charles Wesley fill the heart and soul with joy in response to all we have learned this week about Abraham, who is called "the man of faith" (NIV) and "the believer" (NASB) in Galatians 3:9. Oh that we might be called a person of faith and experience the amazing results of faith! We want to have the kind of faith that will walk on water, experiencing freedom in the midst of turbulent circumstances and terrifying trials. Is it possible? After studying the life of Abraham who left everything, surrendered everything, and emerged triumphant and victorious, the answer is a resounding yes!

As you think about all you learned this week, what is the most important truth and promise from God that will help you live and walk by faith?

REST IN HIS LOVE

"He made Him who knew no sin to be sin on our behalf, so that we might become the righteousness of God in Him" (2 Corinthians 5:21).

A HEART SET FREE

Therefore there is now no condemnation for those who are in Christ Jesus. Romans 8:1
Zion National Park, Utah, USA
Nikon D7000, ISO 160, f11.0, 1/160, Adobe Photoshop, Nik Silver Efex Pro
MYPHOTOWALK.COM—CATHERINEMARTIN.SMUGMUG.COM

DEVOTIONAL READING
BY LILIAS TROTTER

DEAR FRIEND,

This week you walked into God's Gallery of Faith and stopped in front of the portrait of Abraham. Look back over your week of study and summarize what you learned from the life of Abraham.

What were your most meaningful discoveries this week as you spent time with the Lord?

Most meaningful insight:

Most meaningful devotional reading:

Most meaningful verse:

Your most significant promise this week written in A Promise A Day:

It is no strange thing that happens to us if God takes us at our word, and strips us for a while of all that made life beautiful. It may be outward things—bodily comfort, leisure, culture, reputation, friendships—that have to drift away as our hands refuse to clasp on anything but God's will for us. Or it may be on our inner life that the stripping falls, and we have to leave the sunny lands of spiritual enjoyment for one after another of temptation's battlefields, where every inch of our foothold has to be tested, where even, it may seem to give way—till no experience, no resting place remains to us in heaven or earth but God Himself—till we are "wrecked upon God." Earn His beatitude, His "Blessed is he (or she)—the beatitude of the trusting.[13]

LILIAS TROTTER IN PARABLES OF THE CROSS

Viewer Guide

❧ WEEK FOUR ❧

Faith When Dreams Are Shattered

In Week Four of *Walk On Water Faith*, you had the opportunity to study the life of Abraham, the friend of God. He is one of our heroes of the faith in Hebrews 11, God's Gallery of Faith. Today we are going to learn about faith when our dreams are shattered from Abraham. So, grab your Bibles, and let's talk about the amazing faith of Abraham.

"Without becoming weak in faith he contemplated his own body, now as good as dead since he was about a hundred years old, and the deadness of Sarah's womb; yet with respective tot he promise of God, he did not waver in unbelief but grew strong in faith, giving glory to God, and being fully assured that what God had promised, He was able also to perform" Romans 4:19-21

Three times in Abraham's life where he experienced disappointment and shattered dreams:

1. When his _____ died.

Genesis 12:1-5

2. Another shattered dreams was _____for Abraham.

Genesis 15:1-6

3. When God asked Abraham to _____ his son, Isaac.

Genesis 22:1-2

What we learn from these examples in the life of Abraham about faith and shattered dreams:

1. When your dreams are shattered, God is broadening your _____.

Isaiah 55:8-9

2. When your dreams are shattered, God has a _____ for you that He will fulfill.

2 Peter 1:4

3. When your dreams are shattered, learn how to _____ the promise of God by faith.

Romans 4:19-21

4. When your dreams are shattered, develop a deeper _____ to your Lord.

Genesis 12:8

5. When your dreams are shattered, God is developing your _____

and growing your _____.

1 Peter 1:7, 2 Corinthians 4:17

6. When your dreams are shattered, remember your _____.

Hebrews 11:16

꧁ *Video messages are available on DVDs or as Digital M4V Video. Audio messages are available as Digital MP3 Audio. Visit the Quiet Time Ministries Online Store at www.quiettime.org.*

THE FAITH OF MOSES
THE MAN OF GOD

Hebrews 11:23-31

Moses may have had commanding features of mind and body, and have been versed in all the learning of his time, yet the marvelous outcome of his life work was not due to any of these qualities, but to the faith that knit his soul to God.[1]

F.B. Meyer

FAITH THAT LEAVES A LEGACY

By faith Moses, when he was born, was hidden for three months by his parents, because they saw he was a beautiful child; and they were not afraid of the king's edict.

HEBREWS 11:23

PREPARE YOUR HEART

One of the greatest callings in all of life is that of a parent. And probably one of the greatest influences in a person's life is the influence of a mother. Dr. Bill Bright, co-founder of Campus Crusade for Christ, often spoke of the impact his mother had on his life for loving the Lord. And many have read of Susannah Wesley who would stand in the middle of her kitchen with her apron over her head, in prayer and quiet time with the Lord. Her two sons, John and Charles Wesley, were greatly influenced by her godly life. Another less known, but greatly influential mother, was Sarah Edwards, wife of the well-known Jonathan Edwards, a key voice in the Great Awakening of the 1700's. Sarah was mother to 11 children. She loved her husband, was fiercely committed to her family, and demonstrated a life of devotion. She was well known for her hospitality and for sharing Christ with all who entered her home. One biographer has outlined in detail the descendants of Jonathan and Sarah Edwards by their outstanding contributions to society. The marriage produced 13 college presidents, 65 professors, 100 lawyers and a dean of a law school, 30 judges, 66 physicians and a dean of a medical school, 80 holders of public office including 3 US senators, mayors, governors of 3 states, a vice president of the US, and authors of 135 books.[2]

As we continue our more detailed time spent in God's Gallery of Faith, we are going to stop in front of the portrait of Moses, the Man of God. And today we are going to see the powerful life of faith demonstrated by Jochebed, the daughter of Levi, and the mother of Moses.

As you begin your quiet time today, ask the Lord to speak to you from His word.

READ AND STUDY GOD'S WORD

1. Every person has an historical context for his or her life. The same is true for our hero of the faith, Moses. Read the following verses and write what you learn about the historical events surrounding the event of Moses' birth:

Exodus 1:8-22

Exodus 2:1-10

Acts 7:17-21

Hebrews 11:23

2. We learn in Numbers 26:59 that Moses' parents were Amram and Jochebed. Jochebed bore three children—Moses, Aaron, and Miriam. As you think about the bold actions of Jochebed, what impresses you the most about her faith, in light of the times in which she lived? Not only did Jochebed save her son, and nurse him, but then she let him go into the hands of the Lord. She then brought him to Pharaoh's daughter and "he became her son" (Exodus 2:10). Write out your insights.

3. Read Acts 7:20-44 as the story of Moses and write out what impresses you the most today about his life.

ADORE GOD IN PRAYER

Think about the faith of a mother who had no fear and was bold enough to take necessary steps to save her son. Ask God now to give you that kind of faith. Fearless faith is truly a walk on water faith, bold enough to launch out on turbulent waves and see the triumph of God's mighty power.

YIELD YOURSELF TO GOD

When it was announced to Jochebed that she had borne a boy, she was enabled to cast the care of him on God, and to receive the assurance that he should come to no hurt…She put the child into the ark with many a kiss, closed the lid on its sweet face, with her own hands bore it to the water's edge, and placed it tenderly among the flags that grew there. She knew that Pharaoh's daughter came there to bathe, and it might be that she would notice and befriend the little foundling. Or, if not, the God whom she trusted would help her in some other way. Miriam was set to watch, to see "what would be done to him" and Jochebed went back to her house, fighting a mother's natural anxiety by a faith that had enclasped the very arm of the living God, who could not fail her. That is faith. Can we wonder at the faith of a man who was born of such a mother, and nurtured in such a home?[3]

F.B. MEYER IN GREAT MEN OF THE BIBLE

ENJOY HIS PRESENCE

Moses is called "the man of God" throughout the Bible. His mother was definitely a woman of God. How about you? Will you ask God now to give you the kind of faith that makes you a man or woman of God? Will you ask Him for one promise you can hold on to today from His Word? Close by writing a prayer expressing all that is on your heart today.

REST IN HIS LOVE

"So the woman took the child and nursed him. The child grew, and she brought him to Pharaoh's daughter and he became her son. And she named him Moses, and said, 'Because I drew him out of the water.'" (Exodus 2:9-10).

THE FRAGRANCE OF CHRIST

For we are a fragrance of Christ to God. 2 Corinthians 2:15
Zion National Park, Utah, USA
Nikon D7000, ISO 160, f5.6, 1/320, Adobe Photoshop, Nik Silver Efex Pro
MYPHOTOWALK.COM—CATHERINEMARTIN.SMUGMUG.COM

FAITH FOR ALL OUR FEARS

But Moses again pleaded, "Lord, please! Send anyone else!"

EXODUS 4:13 NLT

PREPARE YOUR HEART

Moses went on quite the journey with the Lord. He grew up in the royal courts of Pharaoh in Egypt, being raised by the Pharaoh's daughter. As a grown man, he watched the hard labors of the Hebrews under the cruel hand of the Egyptians. One day he saw an Egyptian beating a Hebrew, and when he saw no one was looking, he killed the Egyptian. The matter became known to Pharaoh who then tried to kill Moses. Moses was forced to flee, and settled in Midian. He was about forty years old at that time (Acts 4:23). He spent the next forty years in Midian, married Zipporah, daughter of Jethro, and became a shepherd. Most men, after forty years out in the wilderness, would be thinking about retirement. And perhaps Moses was weary or settled into thinking his life was nearing an inauspicious end. Little did he know that his greatest task in the plan and purpose of God, was about to be presented to him.

Alone out on Mount Horeb, the mountain of God, Moses was shepherding the flock of his father-in-law Jethro. Suddenly, there in the wilderness, a bush began burning. Moses turned aside to look. We are told that "When the LORD saw that he turned aside to look, God called to him from the midst of the bush and said, 'Moses, Moses!'" (Exodus 3:4). Thus began in earnest one of the most memorable relationships in the Bible—the relationship between God and Moses. It is said that God used to speak with Moses face to face, just as a man would speak with his friend (Exodus 33:11).

In this encounter between God and Moses, you are going to see that Moses has great feet of clay. Alan Redpath has written correctly that "the Bible never flatters its heroes." Oh how true that is especially in the case of Moses. Wait until you see how Moses tried to run from what God was asking of him. Ask the Lord now to show you exactly what He wants you to know in order to grow your own faith today.

READ AND STUDY GOD'S WORD

1. As an overview of Moses' life, read Hebrews 11:23-29 and write out what is most significant to you about Moses.

2. God met with Moses on Mount Horeb and spoke to him from a burning bush. Read Exodus 3:1 - 4:20 as though you are there with Moses hearing all that God has to say. Write out your thoughts about Moses' response to God's request. What do you think were some of the reasons Moses was trying to run from the task God was giving him?

3. What did Moses learn about God in this encounter at the burning bush?

4. It is said of Moses that "he was very humble, more than any man who was on the face of the earth" (Numbers 12:3). We see that Moses did, indeed, go back to Egypt. How do you think the first eighty years of Moses' life helped make him humble? How do you think humility will ultimately help a person have great faith in spite of great fear?

4. What promises did Moses receive when he met with God? And how do you think those promises and his encounter with God helped his faith?

ADORE GOD IN PRAYER

Give me, O Lord, what-er my lot may be,
A heart to look to, and to lean on Thee;
Teach me the thing that pleaseth Thee to do,
And make my life to my profession true.

Let me, my Saviour, on Thy breast recline,
Thy words my comfort, my devotion Thine;
My life's best joy Thy promises to prove,—
Trust in Thy Truth, and triumph in Thy love.[4]

JOHN S.B. MONSELL IN PARISH MUSINGS

YIELD YOURSELF TO GOD

The record is clear concerning Moses: God spoke to Moses and Moses answered. God was conversing with a man! Now why did God single out Moses and perform His will through him? The answer is plain. By his own choice, Moses was God's man. Moses chose to be God's man. God had made His choice first, but Moses agreed to it. Moses made his decision to be God's man, God's servant, God's friend…He deliberately had chosen spiritual treasures from the hand of God above anything this world could offer.[5]

A.W. TOZER IN MEN WHO MET GOD

ENJOY HIS PRESENCE

Perhaps you can relate with Moses. He didn't want to do what God was asking, but in the end, he made the best choice. Perhaps God has asked something of you, it seems impossible, and you feel afraid and faint of heart. How can you possibly say yes, but how can you not respond in the affirmative to your great God, who is Yahweh, the One who is everything you need for every circumstance of life? Moses went to deliver God's message and so can you. How has God spoken with you today? What is His promise for you from His Word? And how will you respond? Write your thoughts in your Journal.

REST IN HIS LOVE

"The LORD said, 'I have surely seen the affliction of My people who are in Egypt, and have given heed to their cry because of their taskmasters, for I am aware of their sufferings. So I have come down to deliver them from the power of the Egyptians, and to bring them up from that land to a good and spacious land, to a land flowing with milk and honey…" (Exodus 3:7-8).

WITH WINGS LIKE AN EAGLE

They will soar high on wings like eagles. Isaiah 40:31 NLT
Zion National Park, Utah, USA
Nikon D7000, ISO 160, f11.0, 1/160, Adobe Photoshop, Nik Silver Efex Pro
MYPHOTOWALK.COM—CATHERINEMARTIN.SMUGMUG.COM

FAITH FOR THE IMPOSSIBLE

By faith they passed through the Red Sea as though they were passing through
dry land; and the Egyptians, when they attempted it, were drowned.

HEBREWS 11:29

PREPARE YOUR HEART

John Yates was a mild-mannered shoe salesman and hardware store manager who lived during the time of the American Civil War. Due to a disability, he was unable to serve in the war, but instead experienced its pain and turmoil from afar. Perhaps he had friends who suffered and others who lost their lives as a result of the war. In 1858 he was licensed to preach in the Methodist church, was ordained, and served for seven years as pastor of the West Bethany Freewill Baptist Church. He wrote of number of poems that caught the attention of Ira Sankey, the singer and composer who served alongside D.L. Moody in his evangelistic ministry. One poem in particular meant so much to Sankey that he wrote the music so the words could be sung by any who needed encouragement in a difficult circumstance. The hymn became known as "Faith is the Victory," based on 1 John 5:4.

Today we are going to look at the faith of Moses in an impossible situation. Oh what hope there is for all our impossibles. John writes, "For whatever is born of God overcomes the world; and this is the victory that has overcome the world—our faith" (1 John 5:4). Your faith is absolutely essential when an impossible storm rolls into your life. Begin your time meditating on the words of this hymn written by John Yates. You might even sing it to the Lord if you know the melody.

> Encamped along the hills of light, ye Christian soldiers, rise,
>
> And press the battle ere the night shall veil the glowing skies.
>
> Against the foe in vales below let all our strength be hurled;
>
> Faith is the victory, we know, that overcomes the world.
>
> Refrain:
>
> Faith is the victory! Faith is the victory!
>
> O glorious victory that overcomes the world.

His banner over us is love, our sword the Word of God;

We tread the road the saints above with shouts of triumph trod.

By faith they like a whirlwind breath.

Swept on o'er every field;

The faith by which they conquer'd death is still our shining shield. Refrain

On every hand the foe we find drawn up in dread array;

Let tents of ease be left behind, and onward to the fray.

Salvation's helmet on each head, with truth all girt about,

The earth shall tremble 'neath our tread, and echo with our shout. Refrain

To him that overcomes the foe, white raiment shall be given;

Before the angels he shall know His name confessed in heaven.

Then onward from the hills of light, our hearts with love aflame;

We'll vanquish all the hosts of night, in Jesus' conqu'ring name. Refrain

READ AND STUDY GOD'S WORD

1. And so now we see that Moses has said *yes* to the Lord and has gone to Egypt in response to God's promise to deliver His people out of the hand of Egypt after 400 years of bondage. Imagine how discouraged and crushed the people of Israel were at this point in their lives. Not only did Moses have to confront Pharaoh, he also needed to meet with the people of Israel and present God's plan. Impossible? Yes, for humans, but certainly not for Yahweh. God is able. If He can create something out of nothing, then He can handle the impossibles of life. Nothing is too difficult for Him (Jeremiah 32:17, 27).

Today you are going to have the opportunity to see how God handled all the impossibles of His people and delivered them from their slavery and set them free. Read the following passages of Scripture and write what you observe about God and His provision and deliverance in every impossible circumstance.

Exodus 4:27-31

Exodus 7:1-7

Optional: Exodus 7:8-10:29 All the plagues that came upon the Egyptians before Pharaoh agreed to let them go

Exodus 11:1-12:51

2. Believe it or not, Pharaoh still changed his mind after each new plague, and finally gathered his armies to chase after the Moses and the people of Israel. But God was about to perform a miracle none of His people could ever forget. The people of Israel were standing on the edge of the Red Sea and God was promising Moses a miracle. He said, "Tell the sons of Israel to go forward. As for you, lift up your staff and stretch out your hand over the sea and divide it, and the sons of Israel shall go through the midst of the sea on dry land. As for Me, behold, I will harden the hearts of the Egyptians so that they will go in after them; and I will be honored through Pharaoh and all his arm, through his chariots and his horsemen. Then the Egyptians will know that I am the LORD, when I am honored through Pharaoh, through his chariots and his horsemen" (Exodus 14:15-18). Moses was faced with a seemingly impossible situation from the human perspective. But all things are possible for God, who is Creator of heaven and earth.

Read Exodus 14:24-31 and write out your most significant insights about how God dealt with this impossible situation.

ADORE GOD IN PRAYER

What are the impossibles for you today? Will you lay out each impossible circumstance before your Lord and ask Him to give you a walk on water faith for each one? You might use a Prayer page to write out your requests. Then, you can write out His amazing answers for each impossible.

YIELD YOURSELF TO GOD

As you envision the Red Sea's mighty walls of water, separated by the outstretched hand of the Eternal in response to the faith of a single man, learn what God will do for His own. Never dread any consequence resulting from absolute obedience to His command. Never fear the rough waters ahead, which through their proud contempt impede your progress. God is greater than the roar of raging water and the mighty waves of the sea. "The LORD sits enthroned over the flood; the LORD is enthroned as King forever" (Psalm 29:10). A storm is simply the hem of His robe, the sign of His coming, and the evidence of His presence. Dare to trust Him! Dare to follow Him! Then discover that the forces that blocked your progress and threatened your life become at His command the very materials He uses to build your street of freedom.

F.B. MEYER IN STREAMS IN THE DESERT

The harder the place the more He loves to show His power. If you wish to find Him real, come to Him in some great trouble. He has no chance to work until you get in a hard place. He led Israel out of the usual way till He got them to the Red Sea. Then there was room for His power to be manifested. God loves the hard places and the narrow places. Rejoice if you are in such a place! Even if it is in the very heart of the foe God is able to deliver you. Let not your faith in Him waver for a moment, and you will find *His omnipotence is all upon your side for every difficulty in which you can be placed.* "When you get in the tight place," says Harriet Beecher Stowe, "and everything goes against you, till it seems as if you could not hold on a minute longer, never give up then, *for that is just the place and the time that the tide will turn.*"

MRS. CHARLES COWMAN IN SPRINGS IN THE VALLEY

Have you come to the Red Sea place in your life,
Where, in spite of all you can do,
There is no way out, there is no way back,
There is no other way but—through?
Then wait on the Lord with a trust serene
Till the night of your fear is gone;

He will send the wind, He will heap the floods,
When He says to your soul, "Go on."

And His hand will lead you through—clear through—
Ere the watery walls roll down,
No foe can reach you, no wave can touch,
No mightiest sea can drown;
The tossing billows may rear their crests,
Their foam at your feet may break,
But over their bed you shall walk dry shod
In the path that your Lord will make.

In the morning watch 'neath the lifted cloud,
You shall see but the Lord alone,
When He leads you on from the place of the sea
To land that you have not known;
And your fears shall pass as your foes have passed,
You shall be no more afraid;
You shall sing His praise in a better place,
A place that His hand has made.[6]

ANNIE JOHNSON FLINT IN BEST-LOVED POEMS

ENJOY HIS PRESENCE

Exodus 15:3 tells us that "The LORD is a warrior; The LORD is His name." Will you rejoice in your great God today? We are told in Hebrews 11:29 that what happened at the Red Sea happened by faith. Oh yes, it takes faith for you when you are faced with a situation so difficult that it looks impossible as you stand on the side of the Red Sea where there is no way out, no way back, and no other way, but through. Always remember, with God all things are possible (Matthew 19:26).

What has God taught you today that will help you with the impossibles in your own life? What promise can you hold on to and carry with you through the day?

REST IN HIS LOVE

"Do not fear! Stand by and see the salvation of the LORD which He will accomplish for you today…" (Exodus 14:13).

ALL THINGS ARE POSSIBLE

With people this is impossible, but with God all things are possible. Matthew 19:26
Zion National Park, Utah, USA
Nikon D7000, ISO 100, f5.6, 1/50, Adobe Photoshop, Nik Silver Efex Pro
MYPHOTOWALK.COM—CATHERINEMARTIN.SMUGMUG.COM

FAITH FOR INTIMACY WITH GOD

Now, therefore, I pray You, if I have found favor in Your sight, let me know
Your ways that I may know You, so that I may find favor in Your sight.

EXODUS 33:13

PREPARE YOUR HEART

Moses experienced God in a way that many never discover or embrace in life. He was intimate with God. He talked with God. We are told that "the LORD used to speak to Moses face to face, just as a man speaks to his friend" (Exodus 33:11). That phrase "face to face" means "heart to heart" and implies close and intimate fellowship. No wonder Moses was called "the man of God." Begin your time meditating on these words by Andrew Murray and ask God to give you the same kind of intimacy with God:

> The man of God! How much the name means! A man who comes from God, chosen and sent of Him. A man who walks with God, lives in His fellowship, and carries the mark of His presence. A man who lives for God and His will; whose whole being is pervaded and ruled by the glory of God; who involuntarily and unceasingly leads men to think of God. A man in whose heart and life God has taken the right place as the All in All, and who has only one desire, that He should have that place throughout the world. Such men of God are what the world needs; such are what God seeks, that He may fill them with Himself, and send them into the world to help others to know Him. Such a man Moses was so distinctly that men naturally spoke of him thus—Moses the man of God! Such a man every servant of God ought to aim at being—a living witness and proof of what God is to him in heaven and on earth, and what He claims to be in all.[7]

ANDREW MURRAY IN THE INNER LIFE

READ AND STUDY GOD'S WORD

1. What was the conversation like between God and Moses? Read Exodus 33:9-23 and record your observations about their relationship.

2. God responded favorably to Moses' bold request. Read Exodus 34:5-8 and write out what Moses learned about God.

3. God gave Moses the Law while he was on Mount Sinai. Read Exodus 34:27-35 and write your most significant insight.

4. Faith is always fueled by what God says about who He is and what He does. These are the "I Am's" and "I Will's" of God, His Promises, and His say-so's. How do you think Moses' experience with God over the years grew his faith in God i.e. his ability to take God at His Word?

ADORE GOD IN PRAYER

Talk with God now about your own desire to know Him. Pray the prayer of Moses: "Let me know Your ways that I may know You."

YIELD YOURSELF TO GOD

The writer of the Epistle to the Hebrews lays bare the secret of the marvels effected by the heroes of Hebrew story. We make a profound mistake in attributing to these men extraordinary qualities of courage, and strength of body or soul. But there was one characteristic common to them all, which lifted them above ordinary men, that they had a marvelous faculty of faith which, indeed, is but the capacity of the human heart for God. Four times over this is cited as the secret of all that Moses did for his people. And what is this faith? It is not some inherent power or quality in certain men, by virtue of which they are able to accomplish special results unrealized by others. It is rather the power of putting self aside that God may work unhindered through the nature. It is, in brief, that capacity for God that appropriates Him to the uttermost limit, and becomes the channel or vehicle through which He passes forth to bless mankind. The believer is the God-filled, the God-moved, the God-possessed man; and the work that he effects in the world is not his, but God's through him.

There are, therefore, these necessary conditions of all true faith:
The sense of helplessness and nothingness.
An absolute assurance of being in God's plan.
Entire consecration, that He may work out His will through heart and life.
The daily food of promise.
A daring to act, in utter independence of feeling, on a faith that reckons
absolutely on the faithfulness of God.[8]

F.B. MEYER IN GREAT MEN OF THE BIBLE, VOLUME 1

ENJOY HIS PRESENCE

How does Moses' relationship with God impress you? What have you learned from your time with the Lord today? How will it change how you walk with God? What promise has the Lord given you to fuel your faith in Him?

REST IN HIS LOVE

"The LORD used to speak to Moses face to face, just as a man speaks to his friend" (Exodus 33:11).

DRAW NEAR TO GOD

Draw near to God and He will draw near to you. James 4:8
Zion National Park, Utah, USA
Nikon D7000, ISO 1600, f5.6, 1/40, Adobe Photoshop, Nik Silver Efex Pro
MYPHOTOWALK.COM—CATHERINEMARTIN.SMUGMUG.COM

FAITH TO PASS IT ON

Now Moses went up from the plains of Moab to Mount Nebo, to the top of Pisgah, which is opposite Jericho. And the LORD showed him all the land…

DEUTERONOMY 34:1

PREPARE YOUR HEART

So there he stood gazing out over the Promised Land, viewing it from afar. He was now alone with the Lord. He had charged the people with blessings and exhortations. He had passed the baton on to Joshua who had believed God for the fulfillment of His promises. And now was the moment for Moses to step from time into eternity. There, alone with his Lord, he saw the land of promise. We can only imagine what went through his mind. He saw it, but couldn't enter it because he "broke faith" with God while with the people and did not regard God as holy "in the midst of the sons of Israel" (Deuteronomy 3:51-52). Moses had been instructed to speak to the rock to bring forth water, but instead he struck the rock (Numbers 20:1-12). These words are tough to take but indicate the enormous responsibility of a leader of God. They also show us just how important our faith is and what it means to God. As His followers, we must walk and live by faith. If He has given us His promises, and shown us His character, then we have been extended a gift of His grace. Let us not idly pass it by. God loved Moses and because of His grace and compassion, He showed Moses the beauty and wonder of the Promised Land. It must have been quite a moment for the two of them together, sharing the view. Perhaps Moses was quiet, too moved to speak. Or maybe he was shouting with joy, giving God praise and worship. We do know that God presented it to him as a fulfillment of a covenant promise. The Lord showed him all the land (Deuteronomy 34:2-3), then said, "This is the land which I swore to Abraham, Isaac, and Jacob, saying, 'I will give it to your descendants; I have let you see it with your eyes, but you shall not go over there'" (Deuteronomy 34:4). And so the curtain falls on our final view of the portrait of Moses in God's Gallery of Faith: "So Moses the servant of the LORD died there in the land of Moab, according to the word of the LORD. And He buried him in the valley in the land of Moab, opposite Beth-peor; but no man knows his burial place to this day" (Deuteronomy 34:5-6). This is not the last time we see Moses in the history of Israel however. For when Jesus went up to the Mount of Transfiguration prior to His arrest, crucifixion, burial, and resurrection, He was met by two of God's men of faith: Moses and Elijah. Ask God to speak to you from His Word today.

READ AND STUDY GOD'S WORD

1. Moses was a man of God who is listed in God's Gallery of Faith as a hero of the faith. His life is followed by two events in Hebrews 11:30-31. Read about these two events in Hebrews 11:30-31 and write out what happened because of faith.

2. Joshua was Moses' successor and he was the one who led the "by faith" adventure at Jericho. Read the following verses and record what you learn about Joshua and Moses:

Deuteronomy 34:9-12

Joshua 1:1-9

Joshua 6:2-3, 15-21

3. Moses the man of God was a man of great faith. And so was Joshua. It takes faith to pass on what God has taught you to someone else. Moses did that with Joshua. Read Exodus 33:11 and note where Joshua was and what he must have learned as a result.

4. Read Joshua 21:43-45 and write out what you learn about God and His promises.

ADORE GOD IN PRAYER

Pray the words of F.B. Meyer today: "O my Father, I know that you love me and that your love has chosen my path. Help me to be satisfied with your wise choice of rough and smooth, of time and tide, of sun and shower. May I finish my course with joy."[9]

YIELD YOURSELF TO GOD

This gave a majesty to the early saints, that they dared to do at God's command things which reason would condemn. Whether it be a Noah who is to build a ship on dry land, an Abraham who is to offer up his only son, or a Moses who is to despise the treasures of Egypt, or a Joshua who is to besiege Jericho seven days, using no weapons but the blasts of rams' horns, they all act upon God's command, contrary to the dictates of reason; and the Lord gives them a rich reward as the result of their obedient faith. Would to God we had in the religion of these modern times a more potent infusion of this heroic faith in God. If we would venture more upon the naked promise of God, we should enter a world of wonders to which as yet we are strangers…nothing is too hard for the God that created the heavens and the earth.[10]

CHARLES HADDON SPURGEON IN MORNING AND EVENING

ENJOY HIS PRESENCE

Oh what a week we have had in God's Word, living with Moses the man of God, one of God's great heroes of the faith. How has God spoken to you from the life of Moses? How does his life help you in your own walk of faith? What promise has God given you today? Think about all you've learned, especially about the great task God gave Moses at the age of 80, the impossible circumstance of crossing the Red Sea, and his intimate relationship of a face-to-face friendship with God. God bless you, dear friend, as you grow in your walk on water faith in the Lord.

REST IN HIS LOVE

"Now Joshua the son of Nun was filled with the spirit of wisdom, for Moses had laid his hands on him; and the sons of Israel listened to him and did as the Lord had commanded Moses. Since that time no prophet has risen in Israel like Moses, whom the Lord knew face to face..." (Deuteronomy 34:9-10).

UNFAILING LOVE

I lavish unfailing love to a thousand generations. Exodus 34:7 NLT
Zion National Park, Utah, USA
Nikon D7000, ISO 160, f11.0, 0.4, Adobe Photoshop, Nik Silver Efex Pro
MYPHOTOWALK.COM—CATHERINEMARTIN.SMUGMUG.COM

DEVOTIONAL READING
BY ANDREW MURRAY

Dear Friend,

You have gazed upon the portrait of Moses in God's Gallery of Faith this week. Take some time to think about all you have learned and write a prayer to the Lord expressing all that is on your heart.

What were your most meaningful discoveries this week as you spent time with the Lord?

Most meaningful insight:

Most meaningful devotional reading:

Most meaningful verse:

Your most significant promise this week written in A Promise A Day:

When Moses went in to pray for himself or his people, and to wait for instructions, he found One waiting for him. What a lesson for our morning watch. A prayerful spirit is the spirit to which God will speak. A prayerful spirit will be a listening spirit, waiting to hear what God says. In our interaction with God, His presence and the part He takes must be as real as our own. We must ask what is needed so that our Scripture reading and prayer may result in true fellowship with God…Any place where we are really alone with God may be to us the secret of His presence…Let us enter the closet, and prepare to pray, with a heart that humbly waits to hear God speak. In God's Word we shall indeed hear the voice of One speaking to us…Prayer and the Word are inseparably linked together. Power in the use of either depends upon the presence of the other. The Word gives me guidance for prayer, telling me what God will do for me. It shows me the path of prayer, telling me how God would have me come. It gives me the power for prayer, the courage to accept the assurance that I will be heard. And it brings me the answer to prayer, as it teaches what God will do for me…Prayer and the Word have one common center—God. Prayer seeks God; the Word reveals God. In prayer, we ask God; in the Word, God gives the answers. In prayer we rise to heaven to dwell with God; in the Word God comes to dwell with us. In prayer we give ourselves to God; in the Word God gives Himself to us. In prayer and the Word everything revolves around God. Make God the center of your heart, the one object of your desire. Prayer and the Word will give a blessed fellowship with God, the interchange of thought, love, and life.[11]

ANDREW MURRAY

Viewer Guide

Faith For All Your Impossibles

In Week Five of *Walk On Water Faith* you had the opportunity to study the life of Moses, the friend of God. He is one of our heroes of the faith in Hebrews 11, God's Gallery of Faith. Today we are going to learn about faith from the life of Moses for all your impossible circumstances. So, grab your Bibles, and let's talk about the amazing faith of Moses.

"By faith he left Egypt, not fearing the wrath of the king; for he endured, as seeing Him who is unseen" (Hebrews 11:27).

What we learn from the five impossibles of Moses:

1. Faith sees _____truth and is not _____
of the impossible.

The _____of God will help you see the eternal and not
fear the impossible.

2. Faith chooses the _____of Christ over the treasure of the world
in every impossible, favoring what lasts _____instead of what
is passing away.

Invest in _____things, not _____worldly
things.

3. God _____our faith by revealing Himself, and what we see
enables us to _____in every impossible.

_____the character of your God is a great secret in
making it through the impossibles.

4. Faith _____God in every impossible.

_____to the Lord is your best step of faith in your impossibles.

5. God will _____the impossible of you so that as you step out in faith, He can _____the impossible.

For God to do the impossible, an impossible situation is _____.

What's your impossible today? Launch out in faith and walk on water!

Video messages are available on DVDs or as Digital M4V Video. Audio messages are available as Digital MP3 Audio. Visit the Quiet Time Ministries Online Store at www.quiettime.org.

THE FAITH OF THE JUDGES

Judges 4-16

Some people assume worry is the result of too much thinking. Actually, it's the result of too little thinking in the right direction. If you know who God is and understand His purposes, promises, and plans, it will help you not to worry.[1]

JOHN MACARTHUR

WHEN YOU NEED TO LEAD—DEBORAH

Now Deborah, a prophetess, the wife of Lappidoth, was judging Israel at that time.

JUDGES 4:4

PREPARE YOUR HEART

Every generation has a handful of leaders who love God and serve Him well. And some are well-remembered for many years after they have gone to be with the Lord. Names like Spurgeon and Moody are not easily forgotten. And then there are others who walked faithfully with the Lord, were well known in their day, but are now, for the most part, forgotten. No one really knows their names. And yet their lives have made an imprint because of their faith in God. We don't realize the remarkable lives they led or the fruit of their work, but it does remain nevertheless. And heaven will tell the real story.

One man who was known in his day as a great leader and man of God was J. Gresham Machen. He was called Mr. Valiant-for-Truth *par excellence* by one biographer.[2] He was a theologian in the early 20th century, Professor of New Testament at Princeton Seminary, and founder of Westminster Theological Seminary. His textbook, *New Testament Greek For Beginners*, is still used today in many seminaries worldwide.[3] In his day, Machen was a voice for orthodoxy, holding to the truth of God's Word, in the face of a growing liberalism. He labored in season and out of season regardless of personal cost and suffered attack and humiliation because of his steadfast position. In the context of great difficulty, Machen wrote his book, *What is Faith?*, "to expound the nature of Christian faith in terms of the teaching of the Bible."[4] God used Machen in his day and time as a faithful witness of what it means to live by faith in God and His Word.

God is looking, always looking, for men and women who will wholeheartedly love Him. 2 Chronicles 16:9 tell us that "the eyes of the LORD move to and fro throughout the earth that He may strongly support those whose heart is completely His." May we be ones who will lead in our generation as faithful witnesses, standing strong on God's promises, and walking by faith in His Word.

We have been studying faith by taking a walk through God's Gallery of Faith. And now, we reach a time in the history of Israel where God's people no longer knew or loved the Lord. They moved from the great victories of faith to the defeat of unbelief. And now they were experiencing the darkness that comes from such a life. In that context, we enter the period of the Judges, mentioned in Hebrews 11:32—"And what more shall I say? For time will fail me if I tell of Gideon, Barak, Samson, Jephthah…"

In this new week of study on having a walk on water faith and discovering power in the promises of God, we are going to turn to the book of Judges, and focus on the promises God gives us for difficulties in life. Each of these people in the book of Judges faced a difficulty or challenge, and in those times, they received promises they held on to and acted on by faith. Ask God to give you the kind of faith, a walk on water faith, that holds to His promises even in the face of great difficulty.

READ AND STUDY GOD'S WORD

1. This week you are going to have the privilege to live in the book of Judges and look at the lives of some men and women of faith called "judges." We see a pattern emerging for the people of Israel in these days where they did what was "evil in the eyes of the LORD" (Judges 4:1). Notice in Judges 4:1 the phrase includes the word "again." And their sin resulted in all kinds of consequences including slavery and oppression. But when they cried out to the Lord, the Lord responded. In Judges 4:3, "The sons of Israel cried to the LORD." In Judges 2:16 we see that "the LORD raised up judges who delivered them from the hands of those who plundered them." Today you are going to briefly look at Deborah, a woman of faith. She was a prophetess and a judge during the dark times in the history of Israel (Judges 4:4). God's people were being oppressed by the Canaanites led by Jabin and Sisera. Sisera's strength was in his 900 chariots and he terrorized the tribes of Israel near the Valley of Jezreel.[5] She was a leader entrusted with the great task of leading. Read Judges 4:4-9 and write out everything you notice about Deborah and her leadership.

2. The Lord gave great victory that day and gave wisdom to Deborah. Read Judges 4:14-15 and write out how Deborah demonstrated faith in God and was used greatly by Him.

3. Deborah was a woman of faith in her time. Read Judges 5:1-4 and note her reliance on the Lord and her love for the Lord. Also, read Judges 5:15-16, 5:21, and 5:31 and note the kinds of things that lead to faith.

4. Look at the following verses and record what you learn when you need help and guidance. Personalize your insights and observations.

Psalm 32:8

Psalm 37:23

Isaiah 45:2-3

Isaiah 58:11

Philippians 4:6-7

James 1:5-7

ADORE GOD IN PRAYER

Pray the words of F.B. Meyer today: "My soul wakes early and turns to you, O God, for the light. Your light is better than life, therefore, my lips shall praise you. Take my hand in yours, and make the crooked places straight and the rough places plain, that your name may be glorified in my daily walk and conversation."[6]

YIELD YOURSELF TO GOD

> No matter how great and good be the Saviour, we cannot trust Him unless there be some contact specifically between ourselves and Him. Faith in a person involves not merely the conviction that the person trusted is able to save, but also the conviction that he is able and willing to save *us*; that there should be faith, there must be some definite relation between the person trusted and a specific need of the person who trusts...It is not enough for us to know that Jesus is great and good; it is not enough for us to know that He was instrumental in the creation of the world and that He is now seated on the throne of all being. These things are indeed necessary to faith, but they are not all that is necessary; if we are to trust Jesus, we must come to Him personally and individually with some need of the soul which He alone can relieve.[7]

> J. GRESHAM MACHEN IN WHAT IS FAITH?

ENJOY HIS PRESENCE

What is your need today? Whatever it is, God has a promise meant for you specifically in the need. Write a prayer expressing all that is on your heart today. Then, write out your needs on a Prayer page and lay each one out before the Lord. Ask Him for a promise to hold on to in the midst of your need. Then watch to see how He answers your prayers. God bless you, dear friend.

REST IN HIS LOVE

"The LORD directs the steps of the godly. He delights in every detail of their lives" (Psalm 37:23 NLT).

THE LORD IS MY STRENGTH

The LORD is my strength and my shield; My heart trusts in Him, and I am helped. Psalm 28:7
Zion National Park, Utah, USA
Nikon D7000, ISO 160, f11.0, 3 Bracketed EXP, Adobe Photoshop, Nik Silver Efex Pro
MYPHOTOWALK.COM—CATHERINEMARTIN.SMUGMUG.COM

WHEN YOU ARE IN A BATTLE—BARAK

Deborah said to Barak, "Arise! For this is the day in which the LORD has given Sisera into your hands; behold the LORD has gone out before you."

JUDGES 4:14

PREPARE YOUR HEART

Sometimes the battle seems to rage, doesn't it? Just when you thought the pressure was easing a bit, something happens to make everything seem that much more stressful. Recognize, dear friend, that you are indeed in a spiritual battle. Warren Wiersbe points out that "anyone who chooses to be on the side of the Lord Jesus Christ will face severe opposition from Satan and his followers. And those who refuse to fight will fall in the heat of the battle…the Christian life is not a playground—it's a battleground. And whether we like it or not, every Christian is called to be a soldier and to 'fight the good fight' (1 Timothy 6:12)."[8] And what is the "good fight?" It's the fight of faith according to Paul in 1 Timothy 6:12. Oswald Chambers points out that faith is a fight always, not sometimes.[9] So if you feel like you are in a fight today, realize you are. And that fight is not about the circumstances, it's about your faith. You need to hear from God, grasp His promise, and live in it by faith with your eyes steadfastly fixed on Jesus.

Begin your quiet time today by asking the Lord to give you what you need to fight the good fight of faith.

READ AND STUDY GOD'S WORD

1. Today we continue our study in Judges by looking at the faith of Barak, who was called by God to go into battle. Read Judges 4:6-9 and note the commands and promises of God for Barak that came to him through Deborah.

2. Read Judges 4:14-24 and write out how the battle was won and Who won the battle. Remember, Barak is mentioned as one of the heroes of faith in God's Gallery of Faith (Hebrews 11:32). How did Barak demonstrate faith in God?

3. We are reminded by God through the apostle Paul that we, too, are in a battle. Read Ephesians 6:10-18 and write out the promises from God that will help you in your spiritual battles. Also write out what you learn about the shield and the sword.

4. Peter also gives a strong encouragement for you when you are in the heat of the battle of adversity. Read 1 Peter 5:6-10 and write out your actions of faith and the promises that encourage you.

Actions of faith

Promises for your faith

ADORE GOD IN PRAYER

What battle are you facing today? Your shield is faith and your greatest weapon is the Word of God (Ephesians 6:16-17). You are encouraged to "pray at all times in the Spirit" (Ephesians 6:18). Take some time now to pray through each item of spiritual armor in Ephesians 6:10-18 as you fight the fight of faith.

YIELD YOURSELF TO GOD

Like the Israelites, we have a tremendous inheritance in Christ. How do we translate that wealth into a daily walk with Him? By bowing. When we bow down before the Lord in worship and pray to Him, then we are practicing our position in Jesus Christ…When we try to walk without first bowing before God, we will walk out of His paths and will lose ground. As a result, we will not be able to stand before the enemy. Before we can stand against Satan and his army, we must first bow before the Lord in prayer and worship and then put on the whole armor He has given us. We wear this armor, not to gain new territory, but to prevent the devil from robbing us of our inheritance. Satan wants to spoil and pillage our wealth and enslave us. But when we stand in the strength and power of the Lord, we will be victorious in our fight.[10]

WARREN WIERSBE IN WHAT TO WEAR TO THE WAR

ENJOY HIS PRESENCE

What is the most important truth and the greatest promise you have learned today in your quiet time? How will you apply it to your life?

REST IN HIS LOVE

"In addition to all taking up the shield of faith with which you will be able to extinguish all the flaming arrows of the evil one" (Ephesians 6:16)

THE BATTLE IS THE LORD'S

The battle is not yours but God's. 2 Chronicles 20:15
Zion National Park, Utah, USA
Nikon D7000, ISO 160, f22.0, 3 Bracketed EXP, Adobe Photoshop, Nik Silver Efex Pro
MYPHOTOWALK.COM—CATHERINEMARTIN.SMUGMUG.COM

WHEN YOU FEEL FORGOTTEN—GIDEON

The angel of the LORD appeared to him and said to him, "The LORD is with you, O valiant warrior."

JUDGES 6:12

PREPARE YOUR HEART

The man lay half-conscious in a hospital bed in the emergency room. His wife sat nearby, lost in her own thoughts. The battle with cancer had been fast and furious. And now, it seemed, he was soon going to be face to face with the Lord. He lay there in a bed alone and unseen by all but his beloved wife. He was, in fact, a well known, bestselling author who had encouraged many in his same circumstance. He was known for his hospital visitations and faithful prayer for others. A woman who was his friend sensed the urgency of the hour. She was busy that day, but heard he was in the hospital. And somehow, through someone, she had gotten the message. And in her heart of hearts, she knew she just had to go see him one last time. She had been studying the life of Gideon and was impressed with one promise that had come from God: "The LORD is with you, O valiant warrior" (Judges 6:12). At the time Gideon heard that promise, he was not feeling quite so valiant. And yet God had given him words that would stay with him for his lifetime. With this promise to Gideon embedded in her heart, the woman drove to the hospital, went to the emergency room, and walked into the small, dark room where her friend lay. As soon as she walked in the room, his eyes opened and he looked directly at her with the hint of a smile. He was surprised to see her. Surprised to see anybody. She looked into the eyes of her friend who was so precious to her. He had been her encouragement to become a writer and impact others with her books. She recognized the look in his eyes and the appearance of his face. She knew, as he did, that soon he would step into the presence of the Lord he loved so much. She didn't know what to say at first. There was just a knowing look between them. And then, the promise from God came to her and she knew it was for him that day: "The LORD is with you, O valiant warrior." He looked into her eyes and smiled. He didn't have to say anything. She knew he knew it was from the Lord for him that day. They spent a few moments together and then his friend prayed for both he and his wife. She looked one more time into those blue eyes that had often sparkled with excitement about some author or some new project from the Lord. Today the eyes were different. They had a far-away reflective look in them, as though thinking and looking beyond the here and now all the way to forever. She walked out of the room. That was the last time she saw her friend. Two weeks later he was face to face with the Lord. And he was a valiant warrior and the Lord was, indeed, with him then and is with him even now.[11]

There are times in our lives when we feel forgotten. Perhaps we have wandered away from the Lord. Or we are be experiencing a trial that is seemingly impossible with apparently no obvious answer. And we feel alone in the storm.

The people of Israel experienced just such a time. They had once again done what was evil in the eyes of the Lord. And now they were experiencing oppression at the hands of the Midianites. We are told that "Israel was brought very low because of Midian, and the sons of Israel cried to the LORD" (Judges 6:6). The Lord responded to the cries of His people and chose a new instrument of deliverance: Gideon. Gideon was a man of faith who felt forgotten in the midst of a people who had wandered far from the Lord.

Today, ask God to show you how you can learn from Gideon and have a walk on water kind of faith.

READ AND STUDY GOD'S WORD

1. God chose Gideon to deliver His people from the hand of the Midianites. Read Judges 6:11-12 and think about those words from the Lord. Write out the promises you notice in the verses. God sees who we will be become as we rely on His strength. (Note that the "angel of the LORD" is thought by most commentators to be an appearance of the pre-incarnate Christ.)

2. In Judges 6:13 Gideon's first response was, "O my lord, if the LORD is with us, why then has all this happened to us? And where are all His miracles which our fathers told us about, saying, 'Did not the LORD bring us up from Egypt?' But now the LORD has abandoned us and given us into the hand of Midian." Describe how Gideon was feeling at this moment. How do you think he was moving from feelings to faith?

3. Read Judges 6:12-24 and write out all that God promised and Gideon's responses, including his final response seen in these verses.

4. Now Gideon is ready to go into battle. Watch how the Lord wins the day and makes Gideon into a man of faith whose name is written in Hebrews 11:32. Read Judges 7:1-9 and 7:19-22 and write out what you notice about God's ways in making us a person who has a walk on water faith.

5. Read the following promises and underline words that encourage you when you may feel forgotten:

Psalm 27:1-3

Isaiah 41:10

Isaiah 49:14-16

ADORE GOD IN PRAYER

Think about the fact that the Lord is with you. Thank Him today for His presence in your life and ask Him to give you strength for every battle, remembering the example of Gideon and how His power is perfected in weakness (2 Corinthians 12:9-10).

YIELD YOURSELF TO GOD

God is looking for a man, or woman, whose heart will be always set on Him, and who will trust Him for all He desires to do. God is eager to work more mightily now than He ever has through any soul. The clock of the centuries points to the eleventh hour. The world is waiting yet to see what God can do through a consecrated soul. Not the world alone, but Himself is waiting for one, who will be more fully devoted to Him than any who have ever lived; who will be willing to be nothing that Christ may be all; who will grasp God's own purposes; and taking His humility and His faith, His love and His power, will, without hindering, continue to let God do exploits.[12]

STREAMS IN THE DESERT

ENJOY HIS PRESENCE

The truth is that God never forgets us. No, not ever. But the fact is, sometimes you may feel forgotten. And so, in those times, you desperately need the promises of God to fuel your faith. What promises encourage your faith today? Write your favorite promise from today in A Promise A Day. How will you live in those promises as you walk on water with your faith? Also, take some time to meditate on the photography and promises on the next page as you close your quiet time.

REST IN HIS LOVE

"Can a woman forget her nursing child and have no compassion on the son of her womb? Even these may forget, but I will not forget you. Behold, I have inscribed you on the palms of My hands; Your walls are continually before Me" (Isaiah 49:15-16).

THE EYES OF THE LORD

The eyes of the Lord are toward the righteous, and His ears attend to their prayer. 1 Peter 3:12
Zion National Park, Utah, USA
Nikon D7000, ISO 160, f13.0, 1/10, Adobe Photoshop, Nik Silver Efex Pro
MYPHOTOWALK.COM—CATHERINE.MARTIN.SMUGMUG.COM

WHEN EVERYTHING IS AGAINST YOU —JEPHTHAH

They drove Jephthah out and said to him, "You shall not have an inheritance in our father's house, for you are the son of another woman."

JUDGES 11:2

PREPARE YOUR HEART

Annie Hawks, a young wife and mother, at the age of 37 years, was busily working at her household tasks. She was filled with a sudden sense of the nearness of God and wondered how anyone could ever possibly live without Him. At that very moment, she sat down and wrote the words of one of the most beloved hymns of all time, "I Need Thee Every Hour." Sixteen years later, she lost her husband, and found comfort in the very words she had written. Annie wrote, "It was not until long after, when the shadow fell over my way, the shadow of a great loss, that I understood something of the comforting power in the words which I had been permitted to give out to others in my hour of sweet serenity and peace."[13]

There are times when all seems calm and then times when it seems as though everything is against you. Either way, you can pray the words, "I need Thee every hour." Meditate on the words of this hymn as a preparation of heart today. If you know the melody you might sing the words to the Lord.

> I need Thee every hour, most gracious Lord;
> No tender voice like Thine can peace afford
> I need Thee, O I need Thee; every hour I need Thee!
> O Bless me now my Savior—I come to Thee.
>
>
> I need Thee every hour, stay Thou nearby
> Temptations lose their power when Thou art nigh.
> I need Thee, O I need Thee; every hour I need Thee!
> O Bless me now my Savior—I come to Thee.

I need Thee every hour, in joy or pain;
Come quickly and abide, or life is vain.
I need Thee, O I need Thee; every hour I need Thee!
O Bless me now my Savior—I come to Thee.

I need Thee every hour, teach me Thy will,
And Thy rich promises in me fulfill.
I need Thee, O I need Thee; every hour I need Thee!
O Bless me now my Savior—I come to Thee.

READ AND STUDY GOD'S WORD

1. As we continue our study of faith in Judges, we are going to look at another hero of the faith mentioned in Hebrews 11:32—Jephthah. Our faith hero had a difficult start and experienced a time when it seemed everything was against him. Read Judges 11:1-3 and write what you learn about Jephthah.

2. In spite of a time when seemingly everything was against him, Jephthah became a leader among the people in the fight against the sons of Ammon. His years on the run had deepened his faith in the Lord. Read Judges 11:4-11 and write your observations about his relationship with the Lord and the turn of events in his life.

3. The people had summoned Jephthah to become their leader. Jephthah committed his position and service to the Lord. Jephthah first tried to negotiate peace with the king of Ammon. Finally, Jephthah appealed to the Lord (Judges 11:27) and the king of Ammon prepared for war. Read the following verses and note what you learn about Jephthah's relationship with the Lord and God's provision for this man of faith:

Judges 11:29

Judges 11:30-31

Judges 11:32-33

4. Jephthah defeated the Ammonites in the power of the Lord. His vow to the Lord was intended as an act of devotion, but, according to many commentators, it actually showed a lack of faith in God's power.[14] Because of his vow, it cost the life of his only daughter (see Judges 11:34-40). Jephthah judged Israel for six years, then died, and was buried in one of the cities of Gilead (Judges 12:7). As you think about the life and the faith of Jephthah, how are you encouraged, challenged, and also cautioned?

ADORE GOD IN PRAYER

Take some time now to draw near to the Lord. Use the words of "I Need Thee Every Hour" as a prayer for all you are challenged with in life today. Ask God to show you ways He is meeting your needs even now. Lay every need before Him and realize today the truth of the promise: "If God is for us, who is against us" (Romans 8:31) and that nothing "will be able to separate us from the love of God, which is in Christ Jesus our Lord" (Romans 8:39).

YIELD YOURSELF TO GOD

> Dear one, you scarcely realize the value of your present opportunity; if you are passing through great afflictions you are in the very soul of the strongest faith, and if you will only let go, He will teach you in these hours the mightiest hold upon His throne which you can ever know.[15]
>
> CHARLES HADDON SPURGEON IN BESIDE STILL WATERS

ENJOY HIS PRESENCE

What is the most important promise you have learned from your quiet time today? Close by writing a prayer in your Journal expressing all that is on your heart.

REST IN HIS LOVE

"What then shall we say to these things? If God is for us, who is against us?" (Romans 8:31).

OVERWHELMING VICTORY

Overwhelming victory is ours through Christ, who loved us. Romans 8:37 NLT
Zion National Park, Utah, USA
Nikon D7000, ISO 160, f22.0, 1/25, Adobe Photoshop, Nik Silver Efex Pro
MYPHOTOWALK.COM—CATHERINEMARTIN.SMUGMUG.COM

WHEN YOU NEED GRACE—SAMSON

Then Samson called to the LORD and said, "O Lord GOD, O God,
please remember me and please strengthen me just this time…"

JUDGES 16:28

PREPARE YOUR HEART

Oh what a week of study we have had in looking at the faith of the Judges. And now, in our last day of this week's study, we are going to focus in on perhaps one of the most famous characters of all in the books of Judges—Samson. His story is so famous there have been movies made and books written. Samson is a colorful character who had a time of failure in the course of his life. But we must remember that he is named in God's Gallery of Faith and found grace even at the end of his life. His story is one of inspiration, challenge, warning, and hope. We must always remember that we are not who we were and we are not who we are going to be. We are in the school of faith and the Lord has taken us on as one of His own. He is the author and perfecter of our faith. And He loves us. We have the promise of eternal life if we know Him. As you begin your time with the Lord, meditate on these words in *Quotes From The Quiet Hour*[16]:

> The greatest opportunity
> That God has ever given me
> Was not when that suggestion came
> To show an easy road to fame:
> Was not the day when fortune smiled
> And claimed me, for a time, her child;
> or yet the chance that I must hold
> To turn some talent into gold;
> The greatest one of all, I say,
> Is now, always here—today.
> Today, my opportunity
> Is just as great as I can see;
> It is my privilege to live,
> To learn, to earn, receive, and give;

To do the little task assigned,
And smile the while, nor leave behind
Regrets or flaw in what I build;
But do the work as God has willed
And see in the small part I play
My opportunity—today.

READ AND STUDY GOD'S WORD

1. As we look at another man of faith in the book of Judges, it's important to notice that the story begins the same way. "Now the sons of Israel again did evil in the sight of the LORD, so that the LORD gave them into the hands of the Philistines forty years" (Judges 13:1). We must learn in these words man's tendency to sin and depart from walking with the Lord. The smallest step can lead to the widest departures and we are going to see an example of that in our hero of the faith mentioned in Hebrews 11:32—Samson. Read about the events of Judges 13:2-25 and write your most significant insights about how the Lord was involved in the birth and the life of Samson.

2. Samson's life and work by God's power is outlined in Judges 13-16. In those chapters we see that the stipulations and call of Samson were "no razor shall come upon his head, for the boy shall be a Nazirite to God from the womb; and he shall begin to deliver Israel from the hands of the Philistines" (Judges 13:5). We see that "The Spirit of the LORD came upon him mightily" and Samson possessed supernatural strength to defeat lions and also the Philistines. We also see that he married a Philistine woman instead of an Israelite. The Philistines used Samson's wife to try and discover the secret to his strength. Through a series of different events the Philistines killed Samson's wife. And now, Samson set out to avenge her death (Judges 15:6-7). And for the next 20 years, Samson brought strength to Israel in their fight against the Philistines. And then came a day that changed everything—he loved a woman named Delilah in the valley of Sorek. Read Judges 16:4-22 and describe what happened to Samson.

3. Samson found God's grace could reach him in his most desperate hour. Samson became a prisoner of the Philistines. What the Philistines did not know is that God is great and rules over all. And God loved Samson. Read the rest of Samson's story in Judges 16:23-31. What is most significant to you? How did Samson experience the matchless grace of God in his final hours on earth?

4. Look at the following verses and write out what you learn about grace:

2 Corinthians 9:8

2 Corinthians 12:9-10

1 Peter 5:10

ADORE GOD IN PRAYER

Pray the words of Amy Carmichael as a prayer of surrender today:

Upon the sandy shore an empty shell,
Beyond the shell infinity of sea;
O Savior, I am like that empty shell,
Thou art the Sea to me.

A sweeping wave rides up the shore, and lo,
Each dim recess the coiled shell within
Is searched, is filled, is filled to overflow
By water crystalline.

Not to the shell is any glory then:
All glory give we to the glorious sea.
And not to me is any glory when
Thou overflowest me.

Sweep over me, Thy shell, as low I lie;
I yield me to the purpose of Thy will;
Sweep up, O conquering waves, and purify,
And with Thy fulness fill.[17]

YIELD YOURSELF TO GOD

God deals with impossibilities. It is never too late for Him to do so, when the impossible is brought to Him, in full faith, by the one in whose life and circumstances the impossible must be accomplished if God is to be glorified. If in our own life there have been rebellion, unbelief, sin, and disaster, it is never too late for God to deal triumphantly with these tragic facts if brought to Him in full surrender and trust. It has often been said, and with truth, that Christianity is the only religion that can deal with man's past. God can "restore the years the locus hath eaten" (Joel 2:25); and He will do this when we put the whole situation and ourselves unreservedly and believingly into His hands. Not because of what we are but because of what He is. God forgives and heals and restores. He is "the God of all grace." Let us praise Him and trust Him.[18]

STREAMS IN THE DESERT

ENJOY HIS PRESENCE

What is the most important lesson you have learned from the life of Samson? How will it help you in your own journey of faith in God and His promises in His Word? How do you need God's grace? What promise has God given you today in His Word? Write it in A Promise A Day. Close by writing a prayer expressing all that is on your heart.

REST IN HIS LOVE

"After you have suffered for a little while, the God of all grace, who called you to His eternal glory in Christ, will Himself perfect, confirm, strengthen, and establish you" (1 Peter 5:10).

THE GLORY OF GRACE

The glory of His grace, which He freely bestowed on us in the Beloved. Ephesians 1:6
Zion National Park, Utah, USA
Nikon D7000, ISO 160, f11.0, 3 Bracketed EXP, Adobe Photoshop, Nik Silver Efex Pro
MYPHOTOWALK.COM—CATHERINEMARTIN.SMUGMUG.COM

DEVOTIONAL READING
BY MRS. CHARLES COWMAN

DEAR FRIEND,

Think about all you have learned this week in Judges about faith. Write a prayer to the Lord thanking Him for all that He is teaching you.

What were your most meaningful discoveries this week as you spent time with the Lord?

Most meaningful insight:

Most meaningful devotional reading:

Most meaningful verse:

Your most significant promise this week written in A Promise A Day:

Nothing but our trials and perils would ever have led some of us to know Him as we do, to trust Him as we have, and to draw from Him the measures of grace which our very extremities made indispensable. Difficulties and obstacles are God's challenges to faith. When hindrances confront us in the path of duty, we are to recognize them as vessels for faith to fill with the fullness and all-sufficiency of Jesus; and as we go forward, simply and fully trusting Him, we may be tested, we may have to wait and let patience have her perfect work; but we shall surely find at last the stone rolled away, and the Lord waiting to render unto us double for our time of testing.[19]

STREAMS IN THE DESERT

Viewer Guide
❧ WEEK SIX ❧

Faith To Get Out Of The Boat

In Week Six of *Walk On Water Faith*, you had the opportunity to study the faith of the Judges and learned the great value of trusting God and His promises in difficult times. Today I want to look at the challenges in the lives of some of the Judges, and how they were able to get out of the boat and walk on water with their faith. Grab your Bibles, and let's dig in more deeply together as we study how to have faith to get out of the boat and walk on water.

"Then Barak said to her, 'If you will go with me, then I will go; but if you will not go with me, I will not go.' She said, 'I will surely go with you'" (Judges 4:8-9).

God is not looking for observers; He is looking for _____.

Five people during the time of the Judges who needed to get out of the boat—their challenges and what led them to enough faith to get out of the boat:

1. Deborah—Called by God to get out of the boat and have faith to _____.

Her challenge to her faith in getting out of the boat was difficult _____ and difficult _____.

Deborah's faith to get out of the boat and lead came from having her spiritual eyes and ears tuned to the Lord and His _____.

2. Barak—Called by God to leave the _____ place and get out of the boat to do the Lord's work in a _____.

His challenge was _____ and _____.

Barak's faith to get out of the boat came from God as he stepped out in willingness, asking for _____.

3. Gideon—Called by God to get out of the boat and have faith to do a mighty _____ in God's strength.

His challenge was that he felt _____, unnoticed, and unequipped.

The secret to Gideon's faith to get out of the boat and dare to do great and mighty things was _____ from the Spirit of the Lord and believing God's _____ in spite of the unfavorable odds from an earthly standpoint.

4. Jephthah—Called by God to get out of the boat and have faith to be _____ in _____.

The challenge to his faith was no earthly _____ and the temptation to bear a grudge, not _____, and even take vengeance against those who had hurt him.

In the phrase "before the Lord" we see that what helped his faith was a deep _____ to God and an awareness of His _____.

5. Samson—Called by God to get out of the boat and have faith to be His_____ and to believe Him for _____after great sin and _____ to accomplish a great task.

The challenge to his faith in God was his giftedness and _____ and, at the end of his life, his challenge was the desperation of great _____ from sin and not going to God for grace and forgiveness. What helped his faith in the end was prayer and God honored that prayer.

Don't stay in the comfort of your boat. Ask God for help, strength, and grace for faith to step out of the boat.

≈≈ *Video messages are available on DVDs or as Digital M4V Video. Audio messages are available as Digital MP3 Audio. Visit the Quiet Time Ministries Online Store at www.quiettime.org.*

THE FAITH OF THE KINGS AND PROPHETS

Hebrews 11:32

Every individual believer is precious in the sight of the Lord, a shepherd would not lose one sheep, nor a jeweller one diamond, nor a mother one child, nor a man one limb of his body, nor will the Lord lose one of his redeemed people. However little we may be, if we are the Lord's we may rejoice that we are preserved in Christ Jesus.[1]

CHARLES HADDON SPURGEON

WHEN YOU ARE GOD'S SERVANT —SAMUEL

Thus Samuel grew and the LORD was with him and let none of his words fail. All Israel from Dan even to Beersheba knew that Samuel was confirmed as a prophet of the LORD.

1 SAMUEL 3:19-20

PREPARE YOUR HEART

You have noticed by now that all God's people of faith had great feet of clay. The Bible indeed never flatters its heroes. Many of God's choicest men and women took wrong turns, made unholy decisions, and ran from the Lord at times. They faltered in their faith and forgot God's promises. They forgot that nothing is too hard for God. They became afraid and discouraged. And perhaps you have even wondered how some could even be in God's Gallery of Faith. After all, Rahab was a harlot. Samson's downfall was his association with Delilah. Moses disobeyed God in the end and was only permitted to see the Promised Land from afar. Though men forget, God always remembers. The Bible reminds us that God remembers we are but dust and knows our frame (Psalm 103:14). God loves us. And He set those men and women of old as examples of faith in Hebrews 11 for all who love and serve Him to read and study and learn and ultimately grow in faith. This should encourage you in your own faith. For at times you, too, have faltered. But you need to know God holds you in His everlasting arms and will not let you go. So take heart, oh person of faith. Today is a new day and God has a promise for you. He has a plan for you. Draw near to Him.

One of God's gracious blessings to His people was the gift of His prophets. Prophets uniquely shared the heart of God and delivered God's message to His people. Prophets reminded God's people of God's promises, His ways and His character. Prophets were called God's servants (2 Kings 17:23). A servant was "a humble subject whose goal was to accomplish the tasks assigned by his master."[2] Certain select prophets were also called men of God (1 Samuel 9:6-10) and experienced especially close relationships with God.

As we continue our journey through God's Gallery of Faith, we are going to stop in front of another room in the gallery, the one mentioned in Hebrews 11:32—David, Samuel, and the prophets. David was a king, Samuel was the first prophet, and then we see all God's other prophets including the major and minor prophets.

One of God's choice prophets was Samuel. Today you are going to have the opportunity to see his faith in action and discover how you can imitate his faith. Ask God to quiet your heart now, and speak to you in His Word.

READ AND STUDY GOD'S WORD

1. In Hebrews 11 God names some people and others are listed generally in a group. When He refers to the prophets in Hebrews 11:32, He singles out Samuel. Samuel was a special prophet among prophets and truly shared the heart of God. God gave Samuel many promises about Himself and His ways, and grew him into a great man of faith. Samuel was the amazing answer to prayer for Hannah who longed for a son, yet was barren. Hannah, a great woman of faith, poured out her heart to the Lord and promised if God gave her a son, she would dedicate him to the Lord's work (1 Samuel 1:11). God "remembered" Hannah, meaning He paid special attention to her and lavished great care and concern on her (1 Samuel 1:19). She did bear a son and named him Samuel (meaning in Hebrew "God has heard"). Hannah kept her promise to God, and once he was old enough, she took him to the house of the LORD in Shiloh. He was dedicated to the LORD, worshiped the LORD there, and ministered to the LORD before Eli the priest (1 Samuel 1:28, 2:11).

God had His hand on Samuel for he was His choice servant. Read 1 Samuel 3 and write out what you notice about God's words and works that helped him become a man of faith. What is most significant to you about Samuel?

2. Samuel was the Lord's prophet, and His servant. God used Samuel to speak His word to the people of Israel. He was also the last of the judges in Israel (1 Samuel 7:15). Samuel was a man of prayer. He prayed for the people and encouraged them in their relationship with God. He told the people, "If you return to the LORD with all your heart, remove the foreign gods and the Ashtaroth from among you and direct your hearts to the LORD and serve Him alone; and He will deliver you from the hand of the Philistines" (1 Samuel 7:3). These were formative years for Samuel, the servant of God.

Read 1 Samuel 7:4-17 and write your insights about the following:

Samuel's acts of faith

The people's responses

God's works

3. The people of God responded to Samuel's leadership and turned to the Lord. However, they easily became afraid and were influenced by the culture around them. One day, they said to Samuel, "Behold, you have grown old, and your sons do not walk in your ways. Now appoint a king for us to judge us like all the nations" (1 Samuel 8:5). How does a man of faith respond to words like that? Read 1 Samuel 8:21-22 and write out your insights.

4. God used Samuel as the prophet to serve during the time of the first king over His people, King Saul. Samuel anointed Saul with oil as the new king over God's people. Read 1 Samuel 12:19-25 and record what you learn about Samuel's faith in the Lord.

5. Saul became the first king at the age of thirty and reigned for 42 years over Israel. During his reign there were many challenges from the Philistines. Read 1 Samuel 13:5-14 and record what happened with Saul and how it may have challenged Samuel's faith.

6. God's Word came to Samuel at certain times during his time of serving the Lord. The Lord told Samuel He regretted making Saul king (1 Samuel 15:11). How does a man of faith respond to such words? Samuel was distressed and prayed to the Lord all night. Anointing Saul as king was one of the memorable times of service for Samuel. And Saul was such a disappointment. Have you ever been disappointed by someone or something in your own life?

7. Samuel may have well thought his entire life was of little significance because of the outcome of Saul. However, just when you think your acts of faith are nearing an end, and things will never the same, you hear something new from God. Read 1 Samuel 16:1-4 and write your insights about how Samuel took new steps of faith and what fueled his faith.

ADORE GOD IN PRAYER

Talk with God about how Samuel has inspired your own faith in the Lord. Ask Him to make you His servant in your own sphere of influence.

YIELD YOURSELF TO GOD

When your faith endures many conflicts and your spirit sinks low, do not condemn yourself…There is a reason for your season of heaviness. Great soldiers are not made without war. Skillful sailors are not trained on the shore. It appears that if you are to become a great believer, you will be greatly tested. If you are to be a great helper to others, you must pass through their trials. If you are to be instructed in the things of the kingdom, you must learn from experience. The uncut diamond has little brilliance, the unthreshed corn feeds no one, and the untried believer is of little use or beauty. There are great benefits to come from your trials and depression. Many people have a comparatively smooth path through life, but their position is not the equal of the tested believer. The one who is much plowed and often harrowed will thank God if the result is a larger harvest to the praise and glory of God by Jesus Christ. If your face is now covered with sorrow, the time will come when you will bless God for that sorrow. The day will come when you will see great gain from your losses, your crosses, your troubles, and your afflictions: *From all your afflictions His glory shall spring, and the deeper your sorrows the louder you'll sing.*[3]

CHARLES HADDON SPURGEON IN BESIDE STILL WATERS

ENJOY HIS PRESENCE

Think about all that God did in and through Samuel during his journey filled with triumphs and tests. And God was near and close with Samuel all along the way. Samuel was a faithful servant all the days of his life. God's Word to Samuel fueled his faith and inspired him to great words and works. God will also motivate you with His Word to launch out in service to Him. How has He been leading you in serving Him in your family, with your friends, and in a church community? What promise encourages you in your life today? Write it out in A Promise A Day. Take some time to reflect on the promise and photography on the next page. Close by writing a prayer to Him expressing all that is on your heart today.

REST IN HIS LOVE

"For the LORD will not abandon His people on account of His great name, because the LORD has been pleased to make you a people for Himself" (1 Samuel 12:22).

GOD'S PEACE

His peace will guard your hearts and minds as you live in Christ Jesus. Philippians 4:7
Zion National Park, Utah, USA
Nikon D7000, ISO 160, f11.0, 3 Bracketed EXP, Adobe Photoshop, Nik Silver Efex Pro
MYPHOTOWALK.COM—CATHERINEMARTIN.SMUGMUG.COM

WHEN YOU LOVE GOD
—DAVID

After He had removed him, He raised up David to be their king,
concerning whom He also testified and said, "I have found David the
son of Jesse, a man after My heart, who will do all my will.

ACTS 13:22

PREPARE YOUR HEART

Alan Redpath was a well known British evangelist, pastor and author. Redpath was pastor of Moody Church in Chicago and, in 1961, received an honorary Doctorate of Divinity degree from Houghton College. He suffered a near fatal stroke in 1964, but recovered and served at Capenwray Bible School in England. One of his notable quotes is, "The conversion of a soul is the miracle of a moment, but the manufacture of a saint is the task of a lifetime." One of his best known books is *The Making of a Man of God*, on the life of David, the man after God's own heart. Redpath had a unique and profound insight into the ways God works in the lives of His people to develop their faith and make them useful in His service. Knowing God and His ways helps us in our response in faith to God.

David is one of those named in God's Gallery of Faith (Hebrews 11:32). And rightly so. He wrote many of the Psalms and experienced an intimate relationship with the Lord. Today you are going to have the opportunity to look briefly at an event in the early life of David, the shepherd boy who became king over God's people.

As you begin your time with the Lord, quiet your heart and think about your own walk of faith. Where are you with the Lord these days? We have been looking at the lives of many heroes of the faith. How has this journey impacted you thus far? Write a prayer to the Lord today expressing all that is on your heart.

READ AND STUDY GOD'S WORD

1. David is truly one of the great heroes of the faith. He was called "a man after My heart" by God Himself (Acts 13:22). Samuel had the privilege of going to the house of Jesse and his sons to anoint the next king of Israel. When Jesse was asked to bring his sons to Samuel, he thought so little of young David, that he left him out tending the sheep. As Samuel looked at each son of Jesse on the search for God's choice of king, he heard God say, "Do not look at his appearance or at the height of his stature, because I have rejected him; for God sees not as man sees, for man looks at the outward appearance, but the LORD looks at the heart" (1 Samuel 16:7). Just think how that promise alone lights a fire to your faith in developing intimacy with God. Finally, David was brought before Samuel. God said, "Arise, anoint him; for this is he." "The Spirit of the LORD came mightily upon David from that day forward" (1 Samuel 16:13).

David did not become king right away. In fact, he continued shepherding sheep. But God was in the process of making David His man to rule over His people. Oh how David loved the Lord. And oh, how his life was about to enter a fiery time of testing. Saul was still king, but was about to lose the kingdom to David. Saul and his armies were fighting the Philistines. The giant Goliath fought on behalf of the Philistines and his taunts had reduced the Israelites to a place where they were shaking in fear. This continued until David appeared on the scene and heard Goliath. Read 1 Samuel 17:37-51 and write in one sentence what you see about David's love for the Lord and his faith in God.

2. Once King Saul saw how much the people loved David, we see in 1 Samuel 18:9 that "Saul looked at David with suspicion from that day on." And as you continue to read in the chapters that follow, you discover that Saul became so jealous he set out to kill David. He and his armies chased David until David had no choice but to escape into enemy territory. During this time, David wrote his heartfelt, desperate words in Psalm 13:1 "How long, O LORD?" Read Psalm 13 and write your observations about how David's faith was tested and how it was growing stronger.

3. It is thought that David was about fifteen years of age when he was anointed by Samuel and became king at the age of thirty. If those numbers are correct, then David waited for fifteen years to experience the fulfillment of God's promise. During that time, God was making David into a man of faith. He was learning many lessons in his faith. One of the results of David's intimacy with God was the writing of at least 73 of the psalms in the Bible. Read Psalm 37:1-11 and write out what David was learning about God and how to walk and live by faith.

ADORE GOD IN PRAYER

Pray the words of this prayer by F.B. Meyer: "Blessed is the one whose strength is in You, my God, and in whose heart are Your ways. May that strength be mine, yet not mine, but Yours perfected in my weakness. May my heart be strong to hope, to love, and to endure."[4]

YIELD YOURSELF TO GOD

In the development of Christian character there sometimes come moments when darkness seems to fall, the sun seems to set, and to the man himself everything seems lost. Other people, observing his life, wonder if he is sinking beyond all hope of recovery…I find it tremendously comforting that the Bible never flatters its heroes. It tells the truth about them no matter how unpleasant it may be, so that in considering what is taking place in the shaping of their character we have available all the facts clearly that we may study them. Here was David, chosen to be king, destined to be master over great lands and wealth, but living in exile and begging bread. Anointed by the Spirit of God was David, but running for his life from his enemies and destitute of all his friends. So often the providences of God seem to run completely counter to His promises, but only that He may test our faith, only that He may ultimately accomplish His purpose for our lives in a way that He could never do if the path were always smooth. It is when problems and difficulties seem to be overwhelming that the man of God learns some lessons that he could never learn otherwise. It isn't easy to walk with God, for the air at that height is somewhat rare. It is pure, but sometimes it is hard to breathe, and faith almost gives up in the attempt to keep pace with God's way with His child.[5]

ALAN REDPATH IN THE MAKING OF A MAN OF GOD

ENJOY HIS PRESENCE

Perhaps you, like David, have held on to God's promises. And yet you are experiencing challenges on every side to all you know about God and His promises. How does the life of David and his faith encourage you today in your own faith walk? David did become king and ruled for forty years. God is faithful and not one word of His promise will fail you (see Joshua 21:45 for how God keeps His promises). What have you learned from David and his faith that helps you have a walk on water faith today? What is your favorite promise from your study today?

REST IN HIS LOVE

"Delight yourself in the LORD; and He will give you the desires of your heart" (Psalm 37:4).

WAITING ON GOD

But those who wait for the LORD, they will inherit the land. Psalm 37:9
Zion National Park, Utah, USA

Nikon D7000, ISO 160, f13.0, 3 Bracketed EXP, Adobe Photoshop, Nik Silver Efex Pro
MYPHOTOWALK.COM—CATHERINEMARTIN.SMUGMUG.COM

WHEN YOU ARE CALLED BY GOD —ISAIAH

Then I heard the voice of the Lord, saying, "Whom shall I send, and who will go for Us?" Then I said, "Here am I. Send me!"

Isaiah 6:8

PREPARE YOUR HEART

She sat in the back of a room with a thousand students listening to a man speak from the platform. He was sitting in a wheelchair, suffering the debilitating effects of rheumatoid arthritis. With pain, yet power and precision, he spoke on the high privilege of being a disciple of Jesus Christ. He was now coming to the close of the discipleship conference and issued a call of commitment. He explained the call from Isaiah 6:8 when God said, "Whom shall I send, and who will go for Us?" He said to the thousand students, "I'm going to speak those words to you. And if you want to respond to Jesus, to be His servant, and go wherever He leads you, then I want you to stand, state your name, and say 'here am I Lord, send me!'" The young girl listened thoughtfully, her heart pounding. She knew this was a moment etched in time for her. She had spent three years of learning about Christ under the watchful eye and serious training of this man speaking from the platform. She had renounced her former life to grow and follow Christ. But this call now was something deeper, more profound, and life-altering. For she knew that to stand meant she could not go back, but only forward, no matter what kind of challenges or difficulties may come. There was no conflict in her decision. When he issued the call, she stood, stated her name, and said out loud, to God and God alone, "Here am I Lord, send me." That one decision in answer to the call of the Lord meant full-time Christian service, many losses, and difficult days of suffering. But it also meant a deeper intimacy with the Lord she came to love with all her heart. And it meant countless hours of joyful, victorious service in His name.

Have you discovered the joy of answering the call of the Lord? Ask God to speak to your heart as you study the call of the prophet Isaiah.

READ AND STUDY GOD'S WORD

1. In the year of King Uzziah's death, God called one of the greatest prophets of all time into service—Isaiah. Read Isaiah 6:1-8. What did Isaiah see and hear? What was his response of faith?

2. Once Isaiah responded, God told him more about his upcoming years of ministry. Read Isaiah 6:9-11 and summarize God's words and why great faith was required on the part of Isaiah.

3. By the time Isaiah was called as a prophet, the kingdom of God's people was divided into the northern and southern kingdoms. Both kingdoms eventually went into captivity under the Assyrian and Babylonian rulers. During Isaiah's time as a prophet, some of the kings over God's people did what was right in the Lord's eyes and others were wicked rulers. Isaiah's message was primarily to Judah and Jerusalem with some words also to the northern kingdom of Israel. While many of Isaiah's words spoke of judgment, he also offered words of hope, and promises of a Messiah who would save God's people from their sins.

Read the following verses and write out the promises that encourage your faith today.

Isaiah 40:28-31

Isaiah 41:17-20

Isaiah 43:18-19

Isaiah 46:9-10

Isaiah 53:4-5

Isaiah 55:6-12

ADORE GOD IN PRAYER

How has God challenged and encouraged you with Isaiah. Do you sense that the Lord is calling you to a deeper commitment? How will you respond? Write a prayer in your Journal expressing your heart to the Lord.

YIELD YOURSELF TO GOD

By any standard one might wish to use, the prophet Isaiah was one of the greatest theologians of all time. He knew God intimately and obeyed him faithfully; he understood God's will clearly and proclaimed it fearlessly. He was a prince, a patriot, a poet; he was an orator, a reformer, a statesman. He was a man of faith, a man who was unsure neither of God nor of himself. He has been called "the king of all the prophets," "the evangelist of the Old Covenant," "The eagle among the prophets," "the Saint Paul of the Old Testament," "the evangelical prophet." So great a man was Isaiah that it is difficult to exaggerate when describing him.[6]

RONALD F. YOUNGBLOOD IN THE BOOK OF ISAIAH

ENJOY HIS PRESENCE

As we continue standing before the portraits of the prophets in God's Gallery of Faith, we have looked briefly at Isaiah, another hero of the faith. And though he is not named in Hebrews, his presence is there in Hebrews 11:32 and, according to both Jewish and Christian tradition, we also find Isaiah in Hebrews 11:37 where he met his death by being sawn in two by wicked King Manassah. Isaiah served the Lord faithfully for at least 60 years. Remember, Hebrews is written to call a weary people to a new and deeper commitment with endurance and confidence to run their race. How does Isaiah's faith encourage you to run your race with endurance today? What promise encourages you to have a walk on water faith? Write it out in A Promise A Day.

Rest in His Love

"He gives strength to the weary, and to him who lacks might He increases power" (Isaiah 40:29).

Everlasting Lovingkindness

But with everlasting lovinkindness I will have compassion on you. Isaiah 54:8 NASB
Zion National Park, Utah, USA
Nikon D7000, ISO 125, f14.0, 3 Bracketed EXP, Adobe Photoshop, Nik Silver Efex Pro
MYPHOTOWALK.COM—CATHERINE MARTIN.SMUGMUG.COM

WHEN YOU ARE BROKEN —JEREMIAH

Oh that my head were waters and my eyes a fountain of tears, that I might weep day and night for the slain of the daughter of my people!

JEREMIAH 9:1

PREPARE YOUR HEART

And now we walk on the landscape of a vista where we are given a view into the heart of God for His people. For in the prophets we are given a deeper view of God because they shared His heart. Jeremiah is known as the Weeping Prophet for he wept for God's people knowing they would ultimately go into Babylonian captivity. God chose Jeremiah to serve Him during one of the deepest and darkest times in the life of God's people. We can learn much from Jeremiah, for we too experience pain and brokenness. And yet, Jeremiah encourages us that we can walk by faith even during these times when our spirit is crushed. Today as you draw near to the Lord, ask God to give you the faith of Jeremiah for all your broken places.

READ AND STUDY GOD'S WORD

1. God called His prophet Jeremiah during one of the most difficult times in the life of His people. But when God calls a man or woman to Himself, He gives the promises of "I Am" and "I Will"—who He is and what He will do—enough of His say-so's to fuel faith for a lifetime. Read Jeremiah 1:1-10 and write out God's promises to Jeremiah contained in His call of Jeremiah.

2. Jeremiah suffered much at the hands of God's people. Jeremiah literally became God's object lesson to the people of God to help them understand what God was saying to them (see Jeremiah 13). God told His people through Jeremiah that He was sending them into captivity (Jeremiah 38:3). Read Jeremiah 38:1-13 and record what happened to Jeremiah as a result of his words to the people.

3. Now following the captivity of God's people by the Babylonians, Jeremiah is broken and crushed in spirit. Read Lamentations 3:1-32 and write out the words that show you Jeremiah is a man of great faith. Read Jeremiah 32:17 and write out what Jeremiah knew about God. What promises do you think fueled his faith the most?

ADORE GOD IN PRAYER

O God, I trust You.
I don't understand
I cannot begin to comprehend
The wisdom of Your way
In my torn and tangled life
But I am steadfastly believing
That Your plan for me today
Must be—
Surely it *must* be
As kind
As loving
As profitable

As Your plan for me
In joyful days now past.
You are the same
Yesterday
And today
And forever
So, dear God
I trust You.[7]

RUTH HARMS CALKIN IN LORD, I KEEP RUNNING BACK TO YOU

YIELD YOURSELF TO GOD

To a sensitive nature it is an agony to stand alone. To many, the sense of being esteemed and loved is the very breath of life. They are so constituted as to require an atmosphere of sympathy for the full efforts of their powers. Jeremiah, tender, shrinking, sensitive, with a vast capacity for emotion, strong to hate, and therefore to love, was not constituted by nature to stand alone. But in this let us adore that grace that stepped into his life and for forty years made him a defended city, and an iron pillar, and brazen walls against the whole land—against princes, priests, and people. He outlasted all his foes, and maintained the standard to life's end. And this marvelous endurance and steadfastness of spirit was nowhere so conspicuous as during the last months of his nation's independence…It is impossible to recite or read this story without admiration for the man who dared to stand alone with God against a nation in arms. Our sole duty is to see that we are in God's plan and doing His work. Then we will leap barrier walls, pass unscathed through troops of foes, and stand as pillars in His temple, never to be removed.[8]

F.B. MEYER IN GREAT MEN OF THE BIBLE

ENJOY HIS PRESENCE

Oh to have a heart and a faith like Jeremiah, that endures through every battle, all disappointment, and in every wave of tears flooding one's soul. That's the challenge of one who lives by faith. Jeremiah truly demonstrated a walk on water faith. And you can, too. Jeremiah watched the people of God taken into captivity by the Babylonians and also endured subsequent captivity himself in Egypt. Perhaps you, too, have suffered because of your faithfulness to God.

Take heart, dear friend. God knows and He is, as He promised to Jeremiah, "good to those who wait for Him" (Lamentations 3:25). "His compassions never fail. They are new every morning…" (Lamentations 3:22-23). What have you learned from Jeremiah to help you have a walk on water faith? What promise has God given you today?

REST IN HIS LOVE

"'The LORD is my portion,' says my soul, 'Therefore I have hope in Him'" (Lamentations 3:24).

THE LORD IS NEAR

The LORD is near to the brokenhearted and saves those who are crushed in spirit. Psalm 34:18
Zion National Park, Utah, USA
Nikon D7000, ISO 160, f10.0, 1/80, Adobe Photoshop, Nik Silver Efex Pro
MYPHOTOWALK.COM—CATHERINEMARTIN.SMUGMUG.COM

WHEN YOU QUESTION GOD —HABAKKUK

Yet I will exult in the LORD, I will rejoice in the God of my salvation. The LORD GOD is my strength, and He has made my feet like hinds' feet, and makes me walk on my high places.
HABAKKUK 3:18-19

PREPARE YOUR HEART

Have you ever been filled with questions for the Lord? Maybe your questions are a result of a difficult circumstance or even a difficult person in your life. Questions can lead to a deeper faith in God if you will open His Word and live in His promises. Today in our final day of study looking briefly at portraits in God's Gallery of Faith, we are going to stop at a portrait of another of His prophets—Habakkuk. As you begin your quiet time today, ask God to grow your faith and feed you with His Word.

READ AND STUDY GOD'S WORD

1. Habakkuk's prophecy occurs during the decline and fall of the Judean kingdom to the Babylonians. Habakkuk has questions for God. And through his questions he arrives at one of the greatest statements of faith found in the Bible. Read the following verses and summarize Habakkuk's questions and lessons he learned in his journey with God:

Habakkuk 1:1-4

Habakkuk 1:12-13

Habakkuk 2:4

2. Read Habakkuk's prayer in Habakkuk 3:2. What impresses you about his prayer? How does that prayer express his faith in God?

3. Habakkuk knew from the Lord that the people were going to be attacked, taken into captivity by the Babylonians, and moved from their homes to Babylon. Read Habakkuk's response in Habakkuk 3:16-19, and note his feelings and his faith.

4. Habakkuk experienced a prolonged time of trouble and could have lived a life filled with worry and anxiety. And perhaps you, too, have been tempted to walk in worry instead of having a walk on water faith. Read Philippians 4:6-7 and write out your insights about the prescription for worry and anxiety. Habakkuk knew this secret and you can know it too.

ADORE GOD IN PRAYER

Pray the words of Alistair Maclean today:
As the rain hides the stars,
as the autumn mist hides the hills,
happenings of my lot
hide the shining of Thy face from me.
Yet, if I may hold Thy hand

in the darkness, it is enough;
since I know that,
though I may stumble in my going,
Thou dost not fall.[9]

YIELD YOURSELF TO GOD

In the midst of his confusion, Habakkuk remembered this: God is holy—He doesn't make mistakes. God is a covenant-keeping God—He doesn't break His promises. God is eternal—He is outside the flux of history…After re-evaluating his problem, Habakkuk began to praise God for His works, trembling at the power displayed in them (Hab. 3:16). He affirmed that he would rejoice in the Lord, even if everything crumbled around him (vv. 17-18). Why? Because God had proved Himself in the past. That's why the Old Testament contains such an extensive history of God's works—so we can know specifically how God has proved faithful. If you have a problem facing you that you don't know how to solve, remember to praise God. Say to Him, "Lord, You are the God who put the stars and the planets into space. You are the God who formed the earth and separated the land from the sea. Then You made humanity and everything else that lives. Although humanity fell, You planned our redemption. You are the God who carved out a nation for Yourself and preserved it through history, performing wonder after wonder for that nation. You are the God who came into this world in human form and then rose from the dead." When we praise God like that, our problems pale in comparison to all He has done. Remembering who God is and what He has done glorifies Him and strengthens our faith.[10]

JOHN MACARTHUR IN ANXIOUS FOR NOTHING

ENJOY HIS PRESENCE

Think about these words of John MacArthur as you reflect on all you've learned from the lives and the faith of the prophets and David, the man after God's own heart. You can see the greatness of your God in each of their lives and how He acted on their behalf even in the midst of great adversity. God is faithful. You can count on Him in whatever you are facing in your own life. Will you follow the example of Habakkuk today and believe God and His promises even in the face of your own suffering or in light of a loved one's trial? What promise has God given you today to stand on and carry with you throughout the day? Write your thoughts and a prayer in the space provided as you close your quiet time today.

REST IN HIS LOVE

"LORD, I have heard the report about You and I fear. O LORD, revive Your work in the midst of the years, in the midst of the years make it known; in wrath remember mercy" (Habakkuk 3:2).

THE LORD ANSWERS YOU

I sought the LORD, and He answered me, and delivered me from all my fears. Psalm 34:4
Zion National Park, Utah, USA
Nikon D7000, ISO 160, f5.6, 3 Bracketed EXP, Adobe Photoshop, Nik Silver Efex Pro
MYPHOTOWALK.COM — CATHERINEMARTIN.SMUGMUG.COM

DEVOTIONAL READING
BY NORMAN GRUBB

DEAR FRIEND,

This week you had the opportunity to study the lives of some of God's prophets and the faith of David to encourage your own faith in God. Look over your quiet times from Week Seven. How did God encourage you and challenge your own faith?

What were your most meaningful discoveries this week as you spent time with the Lord?

Most meaningful insight:

Most meaningful devotional reading:

Most meaningful verse:

Your most significant promise this week written in A Promise A Day:

As you think about all that you have learned this week, meditate on these words by Norman Grubb: "By transmuting our trials into victories of faith, we cooperate with the Great Victor (Christ) in bringing His victory to a defeated and enslaved world. Thus to Christ's followers, who glimpse the glorious purpose and triumph in and through evils and sufferings, the acceptance and endurance of them becomes an adventure of faith. Thus, and thus alone, does the Christian warrior laugh the laugh of faith. If God's gifts are our blessings, and the devil's assaults are also our blessings, what remains to harm or depress us…a realm of life is entered where we rejoice always, in everything give thanks, and in all things are more than conquerors."[11]

Viewer Guide
❧ WEEK SEVEN ❧

Faith To Take The Next Step

In Week Seven of *Walk On Water Faith*, we studied the faith of King David and the Prophets mentioned in Hebrews 11:32. There is much to learn from these amazing heroes of the faith. Today we are going to look at one prophet, Jeremiah, and learn how to take the next step in our walk on water faith. So grab your Bible, these notes, and let's dig in to the amazing Word of God and learn more about faith from the prophet, Jeremiah.

"Your words were found and I ate them, and Your words became for me a joy and the delight of my heart; For I have been called by your name, O Lord God of hosts" (Jeremiah 15:16).

When God speaks, He is asking us to _____out in faith.

What will help us take that next step of faith?

1. _____ faith. Get clear about what it means to live and walk by faith.

2. _____your faith. How are you doing when it comes to walking by faith?

3. _____your faith. Open the pages of the Word of God.

4. _____your faith. Fix your eyes on Jesus.

5. _____up your faith. Stand firm.

6. _____your faith. Always choose faith over feelings.

7. Put _____to your faith. Walk by faith. Every step is by faith.

8. _____ your faith. Spend time with God every day and find times of refreshing from the presence of the Lord.

9. _____ the fight of faith. The next step is not easy and it may be a fight, but Jesus is victor.

10. _____ your faith with power. Be filled with the Holy Spirit.

11. _____ your faith. Jesus is the author and finisher of our faith and will enable us, by faith, to cross the finish line.

Video messages are available on DVDs or as Digital M4V Video. Audio messages are available as Digital MP3 Audio. Visit the Quiet Time Ministries Online Store at www.quiettime.org.

THE FAITH OF JESUS AND HIS FOLLOWERS

Hebrews 12:1-3

All God's gifts are stored in Christ and from the moment we receive Him into our hearts we find the gradual unfolding of every power and blessing stored up in Him.[1]

W.H. GRIFFITH THOMAS

FOR THE JOY SET BEFORE HIM —JESUS

Jesus, the author and perfecter of faith, who for the joy set before Him endured the cross...
HEBREWS 12:2

PREPARE YOUR HEART

Oh what a journey we have had in learning about walk on water faith. We have learned about the kind of faith that defies the discouragement of circumstances from examples of faith like Peter, Abraham, Moses, the judges, the prophets and others in God's Gallery of Faith. We have spent much time living in Hebrews, the sermon written for those who needed endurance for the race and a renewed confidence. For them and for us, the message is that of a new day. Today is the new day for grasping the promises, experiencing God's power, growing in our faith, and running our race. And now, the writer of Hebrews moves from the Gallery of Faith to his main encouragement and strong words for a weary and suffering group of people. He saves his best example of faith for now. And that example is Jesus, Himself, the author and perfecter of your faith.

Today, as you prepare for your last week of study on faith, think about all that God has been teaching you. Write a prayer to Him, asking Him to speak to you and teach you those things you need to know to live a life of faith, a walk on water faith that lives in the power of God's promises, and pleases the Lord.

READ AND STUDY GOD'S WORD

1. After the preacher of Hebrews, in his wonderful sermon, takes his readers through God's Gallery of Faith, he now has the main message of challenge and encouragement to move these suffering people to a new place in their life of victory and purpose. Read Hebrews 12:1-3. What is the Lord saying in these verses. What does He want from you as one who is His disciple?

2. We began our study of *Walk on Water Faith* with Peter. By way of review, what did Peter do in order to walk on the water in the midst of a turbulent storm?

3. Later in his life, Peter wrote a letter to suffering believers (1 Peter). He begins his letter describing our distress with various trials and calls it "the proof of your faith." Through these trials our proven faith is proven genuine, is more precious than gold refined in fire, and has a great result—praise, honor, and glory at the appearing of Christ. Read 1 Peter 1:7-9 and write your own insights about faith and the proof of your faith.

4. Peter also points out that Jesus left us an example of how to suffer (1 Peter 2:21). He shows us by Jesus' example how to suffer by faith. He points out that Jesus "kept entrusting Himself to Him who judges righteously; and He Himself bore our sins in His body on the cross, so that we might die to sin and live to righteousness" (1 Peter 2:23-24). When you read the Gospel accounts of Jesus' crucifixion you catch just a glimpse of His suffering. For example, we see that Pilate took Jesus and scourged Him (John 19:1). He was taunted and ridiculed by the soldiers, who placed a crown of thorns on His head. He was crucified, nailed to a cross. With these truths in mind, think about what the writer of Hebrews says about how Jesus was able to endure the cross. Often, in our own suffering, we are close to giving up. Here, dear friend, is a great secret to a walk on

water faith. And we learn it from Jesus Himself. "For the joy set before Him endured the cross." What was that "joy set before Him?" Write your thoughts in the space provided.

5. In heaven we will realize completely all that the joy set before Jesus included. Read the following verses and write out your insights of some of the joys as a result of Christ's death on the cross.

Isaiah 53:5

Luke 12:32

Luke 23:43

John 14:1-3

Ephesians 1:18

Philippians 2:8-11

Revelation 22:1-5

ADORE GOD IN PRAYER

I thank You, Heavenly Father, that I know You in Jesus Christ our Lord. He is the brightness of Your glory, the express image of Your Person In His face I see Your face. I humbly ask that the Holy Spirit may open my eyes more fully to see, and my heart more ardently to love, You in Him.[2]

F.B. MEYER IN DAILY PRAYERS

YIELD YOURSELF TO GOD

If anybody faced obstacles on the road of life, it was our Lord Jesus Christ. He was born into a poor family, a member of a rejected minority race. He grew up in obscurity in a little town that was mentioned only in scorn—"Can any good thing come out of Nazareth?" He gathered about Him a small group of nondescript men, and one of them became a traitor and sold Him for the price of a slave. He was called a liar, a glutton, a drunkard, a man in league with the devil. Men twisted His words and questioned His motives, yet Jesus Christ continued to do the will of God. Finally, He came to that greatest stone of all—being crucified like a common thief. But He continued to climb that mountain, and God gave Him the victory. This is why the writer of the Book of Hebrews urges us to look to Jesus Christ and keep on trusting. "Looking unto Jesus the author and finisher of our faith; who for the joy that was set before him endured the cross, despising the shame, and is set down at the right hand of the throne of God" (12:2). We are to look not at ourselves, our circumstances, our troubles, or the bumps in the road, but unto Jesus.[3]

WARREN WIERSBE IN THE BUMPS ARE WHAT YOU CLIMB ON

Never question whether God's bounty can provide food, drink, and clothing, for He has promised you a crown and a mansion. "Do not fear, little flock, for it is your Father's good pleasure to give you the kingdom" (Luke 12:32). Surely He who takes the trouble to give you a kingdom will not let you starve on the road to it. Do not worry about your losses, for "it is your Father's good pleasure to give you the kingdom." Affairs of heaven draw my mind from the paltry things of earth. Heir of heaven, you cannot afford to worry about the little annoyances of this fleeting life. Anxiety dishonors God. I heard about a street sweeper who worked with great diligence. He had a valuable broom that he highly prized, and the few pennies that he spent to purchase it were of great importance. One day a lawyer tapped him on the shoulder and said, "My good friend, is your name so and so?" "Yes, it is." "Did your father live in such and such a place?" "He did." Then I have the pleasure of informing you that you have inherited an estate worth over a million pounds a year." The street sweeper walked away without his broom…Christian, let me tug your sleeve and tell you about a possession that may well turn you away from your present paltry pickings. Jesus Christ informs you, "It is your Father's good pleasure to give you the kingdom," and this kingdom is worth infinitely more than all the gold of this world. You can say, "Let others worry about earthly things, I am going to inherit a kingdom. I will look for that inheritance and will begin to rejoice in it.

CHARLES HADDON SPURGEON

Faith allows you to skip ahead and see that glorious day when you are no longer in the tunnel.

GEORGE O. WOOD IN A PSALM IN YOUR HEART

ENJOY HIS PRESENCE

Think now about the example of Jesus for faith in your own race in life. What difficulties and even impossibilities are you asked to endure to make it across the finish line? What joys are set before you that you can focus on as you run your race? Think about all the promises you have in God's Word including the promises of eternal life. What is your favorite promise from today's quiet time (be sure to write it in A Promise A Day)? Write your insights in the space provided. You may even want to close by writing a prayer to the Lord expressing all that is on your heart today.

REST IN HIS LOVE

"They will see His face, and His name will be on their foreheads. And there will not longer be any night; and they will not have need of the light of a lamp nor the light of the sun, because the Lord God will illumine them; and they will reign forever and ever" (Revelation 22:4-5).

A PLACE FOR YOU

I go to prepare a place for you. John 14:2
Zion National Park, Utah, USA
Nikon D7000, ISO 160, f11.0, 3 Bracketed EXP, Adobe Photoshop, Nik Silver Efex Pro
MYPHOTOWALK.COM—CATHERINEMARTIN.SMUGMUG.COM

RUN THE RACE SET BEFORE YOU

Therefore, since we have so great a cloud of witnesses surrounding us, let us also lay aside every encumbrance and the sin which so easily entangles us, and let us run with endurance the race that is set before us.

HEBREWS 12:1

PREPARE YOUR HEART

In his book, *The Master Plan of Evangelism*, Robert Coleman describes the methods of Jesus. His plan was one of multiplication, not simple addition. Jesus poured His life and teachings into a select few who became His disciples, and taught them to follow Him. Jesus, when He called His disciples, said, "Follow Me, and I will make you fishers of men" (Matthew 4:19). As fishers of men, these disciples learned to take the things they had learned and "entrust these to faithful men who will be able to teach others also" (2 Timothy 2:2). Disciples are constantly making disciples.

And as we read through the rest of the New Testament following the Gospels, we see these disciples, beginning in Acts, running the race set before them—making disciples, fighting the fight of faith, relying on the Holy Spirit, and growing deeper in their intimate walk with the Lord Jesus Christ.

Today, in your quiet time, you are going to have the opportunity to read some of the words of these blessed first century followers of Christ and gain wisdom in running the race set before you. Remember, the story doesn't end with God's Gallery of Faith in Hebrews 11. According to Hebrews 12:1-3, there is a race set before you. And you must run, dear friend. You must run with endurance. Ask God to quiet your heart and speak in His Word today to you.

READ AND STUDY GOD'S WORD

1. Hebrews 12:1-3 gives the picture of a race. It is "the race set before you" implying the plan and purpose God uniquely has for your life (see Jeremiah 29:11 and Ephesians 2:10). And in that race what we look at and how we run will determine the outcome. The same was true for those first century followers of Jesus. Read the following verses and write out what you learn that will help you run with endurance the race set before you:

Acts 20:32

Romans 12:1-2

Ephesians 5:18

James 1:2-4

James 5:16

1 Peter 3:14-15

1 Peter 4:12-14

1 Peter 5:8-10

2 Peter 3:18

1 John 1:1-4

2. In running the race set before you, two hindrances to faith in Hebrews 12:1 are encumbrances and sin. An encumbrance is a burden or a weight. Describe things in your life that can be an encumbrance, hindering your ability to run your race.

3. Sin includes disobedience to God's commands, unbelief, prayerlessness, and deeds of the flesh such as immorality, impurity, sensuality, idolatry, sorcery, enmities, strife, jealousy, outbursts of anger, disputes, dissensions, factions, envy, drunkenness, and carousing (all listed in Galatians 5:19-21). Read 1 John 1:9 and write out how we are to handle sin. How do sins like this keep us from running our race by faith?

4. In Hebrews 12:1 we see that we are to lay aside every encumbrance and the sin which so easily entangles us (following the examples of those in God's Gallery of Faith). To "lay aside" means to renounce and get rid of. How has God been working in your life through this study to help you lay aside encumbrances and sin and run your race by faith? Is there still something—a weight or burden or sin—that you are holding on to and need to lay at the feet of Jesus that is hindering you from running your race?

5. The writer of Hebrews says to run your race with "endurance." Endurance is the spirit which bears things not with passive resignation but with blazing hope, knowing that everything you bear is leading to a great goal of glory.[4] Like Jesus, you may be utterly abandoned by all earthly supports,

yet, through faith in Jesus, you can run your race with endurance, experiencing God's plans and purpose for you. How do the truths you've learned help you to run your race with endurance?

ADORE GOD IN PRAYER

What is the race set before you, dear friend? And how are you running? Do you have sin you need to confess or an encumbrance that needs to be laid aside (Hebrews 12:1). Ask the Lord for everything you need to run your race. Pray that He will fill you with the Holy Spirit.

YIELD YOURSELF TO GOD

> In summary, in (Hebrews) 11:1-12:3 faith is shown to be an orientation to the future. The forward-looking character of faith lends solidness to the realm of Christian hope. Faith celebrates now the reality of future blessings which are certain because they are grounded in the promise of God. For the Christian it is the future, not the past, that molds the present, The preacher confesses, and promotes, the intensity of faith as an effective force which directs Christian life to the future. For the person of committed faith, the future is no longer insecure. The themes of pilgrimage, of sighting the goal but not attaining it, and of refusing to be satisfied with a worldly reward permit the writer to explore the relationship between faith and hope. He understands that a mind is capable of hoping because its consciousness can be shaped by an invisible, heavenly reality…Committed faith holds on to the promise, even when the integrity of the promise is called into question by the evidence of harsh circumstances. Faith knows that the One who promised is Himself faithful.[5]
>
> WILLIAM LANE IN HEBREWS, A CALL TO COMMITMENT

ENJOY HIS PRESENCE

What is your most significant insight from your quiet time today that will help you run the race set before you? Is there any promise in God's Word from your study today that gives you power to have a walk on water faith to run your race?

REST IN HIS LOVE

"But grow in the grace and knowledge of our Lord and Savior Jesus Christ" (2 Peter 3:18).

THE STEPS OF THE GODLY

The LORD directs the steps of the godly; He delights in every detail of their lives. Psalm 37:23 NLT
Zion National Park, Utah, USA
Nikon D7000, ISO 160, f13.0, 1/50, Adobe Photoshop, Nik Silver Efex Pro
MYPHOTOWALK.COM—CATHERINEMARTIN.SMUGMUG.COM

THE WOMEN OF FAITH

Now the women who had come with Him out of Galilee
followed, and saw the tomb and how his body was laid.
LUKE 23:55-56

PREPARE YOUR HEART

The phone rang and when the young woman answered the phone, she couldn't believe the voice she heard. "This is Vonette Bright. And I'm just calling to tell you how much your book has encouraged me at this time in my life." The woman was so encouraged with those words. Vonette Bright was one of her heroes of the faith. The words couldn't have come at a better time, for this young woman was feeling discouraged and thought she may not ever write another book. To hear those words gave her a renewed vitality and encouragement of her own personal calling and mission from the Lord.

The Bible is filled with women of faith and God has given us incredible examples of women who are running their race fully fixed on the promises of God. Vonette Zachary Bright is one of the names listed in the book, *100 Christian Women Who Changed the 20th Century*. And that's what happens when a woman steps out in faith. Things change. People are transformed. Vonette and Bill Bright married in 1948. She relates, "This began the greatest adventure of my life…"[6] While in seminary, Bill Bright received the calling from the Lord to begin Campus Crusade for Christ. Excitedly, he told Vonette. How would she respond? Vonette, the great woman of faith, without hesitation acknowledged it was truly from the Lord and she wanted to be a part of it. In the beginning of the ministry, the Brights lived with Henrietta Mears and received great encouragement from Mears, another great woman of faith. Vonette and Henrietta Mears became great friends. Two sons were born to Bill and Vonette during those days. Vonette grew in her relationship with the Lord as she served faithfully, side by side, with her husband. Vonette Bright has authored many books, spoken at many conferences, and was named the 1995 Christian Woman of the Year. God has used this one woman to touch millions of lives for Christ. Oh what a difference one woman of faith can make.

The Bible is filled with women of faith who loved God and made a difference in the world where they lived. Ask God now to speak to you as you look at some women of faith in your quiet time today.

READ AND STUDY GOD'S WORD

1. As Jesus went from village preaching and teaching He was accompanied by the twelve disciples. There were also women named as His followers. Read Luke 8:1-3 and write the names of some of these women.

2. When Jesus was crucified. His mother, Mary, and others looked on with shock and horror. Matthew tells us that "many women were looking from a distance, who had followed Jesus from Galilee while ministering to Him" (Matthew 27:55). Some of these women were bold in their faith. Reading the following verses and write out what you see about their faith:

Matthew 27:59-61

Matthew 28:1-9

John 20:1-18

3. Women played a very important role in the early church following Christ's resurrection. Read the following verses and record what you learn about these women of faith:

Acts 1:14

Acts 13:50

Acts 16:14

Acts 17:4

Acts 18:1-3, 1 Corinthians 16:19

ADORE GOD IN PRAYER

What does God want for you in your faith today? Turn to your prayer pages and write out some of your greatest requests related to your needs and desire for faith. Also, take some time to look at how God has been answering your prayers and record those answers on your prayer pages.

YIELD YOURSELF TO GOD

We can learn to live by faith when we realize that our faith is in a Person. The person of Jesus Christ provides us a source of confidence that guides our life and anchors our faith. Too many people find all their confidence in knowledge, and yet our finite minds can never understand the true depth of faith. It seems the more we know about faith the less we understand. I can write to you today with a different level of confidence in my faith than was possible a few months ago. My faith sustained me through days and nights of the declining health of my husband while we were in the process of passing the mantle of leadership of Campus Crusade for Christ on to the next generation. I can tell you with confidence that when your faith is placed totally in Christ, and Christ alone, you find purpose in every moment on this earth and look excitedly toward the fulfillment of your faith for all eternity.[7]

VONETTE BRIGHT IN IN HIS HANDS

ENJOY HIS PRESENCE

Vonette Bright defines faith as "believing in that which is humanly impossible apart from a supernatural work of God." What have you learned today from your quiet time that helps you have a walk on water faith that believes in a supernatural work of God? What promise will you hold onto today from the Lord? Write your thoughts in your Journal and your promise in A Promise A Day.

REST IN HIS LOVE

"Mary Magdalene came, announcing to the disciples, 'I have seen the Lord,'" (John 20:18).

THE BLESSING OF BELIEVING

Blessed is she who believed. Luke 1:45
Zion National Park, Utah, USA
Nikon D7000, ISO 160, f10.0, 1/40, Adobe Photoshop, Nik Silver Efex Pro
MYPHOTOWALK.COM—CATHERINEMARTIN.SMUGMUG.COM

FIGHT THE FIGHT OF FAITH
—PAUL

Fight the good fight of faith…
1 TIMOTHY 6:12

PREPARE YOUR HEART

Joni Eareckson was the keynote speaker. She had been serving many years and was speaking to a new generation of believers. Many had never heard the story of her faith—how she became a quadriplegic as a teenager after diving off a pier in the Chesapeake Bay. Her suffering led to a deep journey of faith and she became a Christian. Sitting in the audience that day was a young woman who had read all of Joni's books and was deeply impacted by her faith in Christ. And so, that day, she sat, listening to Joni's words with tears flowing down her face. The years had served to take the listening woman on a road of deep suffering. Joni was her hero of the faith and reminded her again of the need to be "steadfast, immovable, always abounding in the work of the Lord" (1 Corinthians 15:58). As the young woman left that day, she saw Joni being lifted into her van. She saw it as a moment of opportunity given by the Lord, ran to the van, and said to Joni, "Thank you for being faithful to the Lord all these years." Their eyes met for a brief moment, and grateful joy lit up Joni's face. She replied, "Thank you." Later that day, the young woman received a gift of a Bible. Joni had signed it with a pen held in her mouth, and the verse she added to her name was Acts 20:24—"But I do not consider my life of any account as dear to myself, so that I may finish my course and the ministry which I received from the Lord Jesus, to testify solemnly of the gospel of the grace of God." Those words became a personal reminder from Joni to the young woman in subsequent years of intense ministry to finish the course well.

Those words in Acts 20:24 are the words of Paul, the apostle whose letters dominate the New Testament of our Bibles. He was a Pharisee of Pharisees, schooled in the law, and a persecutor of Christians. He was also chosen by Jesus to be the apostle to the Gentiles. One day, Jesus met him on the Damascus road as he was on another mission to arrest Christians. Instead, he was arrested by Jesus, and saved by the blood of the Lamb. Once Paul was saved by Christ, he became a missionary and preacher of God's magnificent grace offered in full measure to all so they might be forgiven and receive eternal life. In the course of his ministry, Paul suffered greatly. In fact, Jesus said of Paul, "…he is a chosen instrument of Mine, to bear My name before the Gentiles and kings and the sons of Israel; for I will show him how much he must suffer for My name's sake" (Acts 9:15-16). Paul suffered and he was a man of great faith. He wrote often about faith and his letter to the Romans is one of the greatest treatises ever written on faith.

Today, you are going to look briefly at Paul and learn about fighting the fight of faith. Ask God to speak to you heart from His Word.

READ AND STUDY GOD'S WORD

1. Oswald Chambers has said that faith is "a fight always, not sometimes" and explains that circumstances actually educate our faith and make the object of our faith real.[8] Every time we step out in faith, believing God and His promises, we experience God's faithfulness, His power, and His mighty work on our behalf. God is able to do immeasurably more than all we ask or imagine according to the power that is at work in us (Ephesians 3:20).

Read the following words of Paul and write what you learn that will help you in fighting the fight of faith:

Acts 20:24

Romans 5:1-5

Romans 8:31-39

Romans 10:17

1 Corinthians 2:9-10

2 Corinthians 4:16-18

Ephesians 3:20

Philippians 1:21, 3:7-8

Colossians 3:1-3

2. Paul encouraged Timothy to "fight the good fight of faith" (1 Timothy 6:12). Paul saw it as a good fight. Don't ever forget that. And in another letter to his disciple, Timothy, he shared words we all would love to be able to say near the end of our life. Read 2 Timothy 4:7-8 and write your most significant insight about these words from Paul.

ADORE GOD IN PRAYER

Talk with God today about the impact of the words of Paul for your own fight of faith.

YIELD YOURSELF TO GOD

> Just when you stand in the conflict, there is your place.
> Just when you think you are useless, hide not your face.
> God placed you there for a purpose, Whate'er it be;
> Think He has chosen you for it; work loyally.
> Put on your armor! Be faithful at toil or rest!
> Whate'er it be, never doubting God's way is best.
> Out in the fight or on lookout, stand firm and true;
> This is the work that your Master gives you to do.[9]

STREAMS IN THE DESERT

ENJOY HIS PRESENCE

What are the steps of faith you need to take today? What can you learn from the example of Paul that will help you fight the fight of faith? What promise is your favorite from the Lord today?

REST IN HIS LOVE

"But I do not consider my life of any account as dear to myself, so that I may finish my course and the ministry which I received from the Lord Jesus, to testify solemnly of the gospel of the grace of God" (Acts 20:24).

I CAN DO ALL THINGS

I can do all things through Him who strengthens me. Philippians 4:13
Zion National Park, Utah, USA
Nikon D7000, ISO 100, f11.0, 1/10, Adobe Photoshop, Nik Silver Efex Pro
MYPHOTOWALK.COM—CATHERINEMARTIN.SMUGMUG.COM

YOUR LIFE SPEAKS, SO FIX YOUR EYES ON JESUS

Fixing our eyes on Jesus…for consider Him who has endured such hostility by sinners against Himself, so that you will not grow weary and lose heart.

HEBREWS 12:2-3

PREPARE YOUR HEART

Your life can speak well beyond your own lifetime, even in the years following your moment of stepping into heaven, face to face with the Lord Jesus. The writer of Hebrews wrote about Abel in Hebrews 11:4 and said that "through faith, though he is dead, he still speaks." Do you hear those words today? Your life speaks, dear friend. And what message is being given by your life? Professor James Stewart, a New Testament scholar in Edinburgh, Scotland, wrote, "If we could but show the world that being committed to Christ is no tame, humdrum, sheltered monotony— but the most exciting adventure the human spirit can ever know, those who have been standing outside the Church and looking askance at Christ will come crowding in to pay allegiance, and we may well expect the greatest spiritual revival since Pentecost."[10]

Think about any of the great men and women of God you have ever heard about. Their lives have a powerful message for you, don't they? You either read their books or have heard them speak. Just think about Billy Graham, who conducted evangelistic crusades, and shared the gospel with men and women worldwide. Only heaven will tell the story of the countless souls that have been saved as a result. Oh what a message is spoken by his life.

On this, our last day of study on faith, let's think together about the message of your life. What will make the difference in the message that is spoken? One thing and that is where your eyes are fixed. Are you fixed on Jesus as you run your race or are you distracted by the people and things of the world? Your life is speaking even now, dear friend, to the lives around you. And everything makes a difference in that message—like your quiet time, the importance of God's Word to you, your life of prayer, your moment by moment decisions behind closed doors—everything is important. You matter to God. You are precious to Him. The most important decisions you can make are the ones that take your eyes away from distractions that pull you away from God or move your eyes to be more firmly fixed on Jesus. What will it be? That was really the message in

Hebrews that the preacher longed for his readers to "get" once they had walked through God's Gallery of Faith. Run your race with endurance and fix your eyes on Jesus. Write a prayer to the Lord, expressing all that is on your heart today related to the message of your life.

READ AND STUDY GOD'S WORD

1. In our last day of study together, take a few moments to read the encouragement from the writer of Hebrews 12:1-3. What is significant to you in those words today?

2. Every day the greatest time you can spend is the time you take alone with your Lord, gazing at His beauty and talking together with Him in fellowship. Read Mark 6:31 and John 15:1-11 and write your most significant thoughts about His invitation to you.

3. What are the greatest challenges to time alone with the Lord and staying close to the Lord? How might these challenges be a testing of your faith and how is faith involved in spending time alone with the Lord? How can you overcome those challenges?

4. Your life has a message and oh, what a message it is when you are walking with the Lord.

When people saw the disciples, they observed their confidence and understood that they were uneducated and untrained men. The Bible then says that the people looking on "were amazed, and began to recognize them as having been with Jesus" (Acts 4:13). Read the following verses and write what you learn about the message given through your life.

2 Corinthians 2:14-15

2 Corinthians 3:1-6

2 Corinthians 5:20

5. The race you run, the life you lead, and the message given by Christ in and through you will have amazing results. Think about the great heroes of the faith and the results of their lives. Just imagine the prayers that God answers as you pray by faith, the people who come to Christ as you share Him with others, others who are comforted as you encourage them by faith, and the incredible plan that God accomplishes in and through you by faith. Be willing to set aside the many things for the "one thing" of knowing Christ and making Him known by faith. When you hear those words "well done good and faithful servant," you will know it was worth it all! What does it mean to you today to know there is a message from your life and results of your faith?

ADORE GOD IN PRAYER

So teach me, Lord, to number
The moments as they fly,—
So teach me, Lord, to Thee to live
That I to Thee may die;

That all my powers, all my praise
To Thee may first be giv'n,
All my talents, all my days
Be consecrate to Heav'n!

Make me remember Whose I am,
And Whom I ought to serve,
How much of mercy I receive,
How little I deserve!
Unite my heart, O Lord!
to fear and reverence Thy Name,
And let my life each passing year
Thy faithfulness proclaim.

Then be my Guard, my Guide through life,
In death my firmest Friend,
My Strength along the rugged way,
My Glory at the end!
And teach me so to number, Lord,
The moments as they fly,
That I may live upon Thy word,
And in Thy faith may die.[11]

JOHN MONSELL IN PARISH MUSINGS

YIELD YOURSELF TO GOD

Heaven and earth will pass away, but God's Word will not. This means that no matter how I feel or what I experience, I can choose to depend on the Word of God as the unchanging reality of my life…The crises in our lives come in varying degrees, from small difficulties to major conflicts. Whether we're faced with the normal ups and downs of life or the most devastating circumstances we've ever encountered, we need to remember that life's difficulties can turn out to be God's greatest supernatural blessings for us—if we are willing to objectify our experiences and trust Him in the midst of them…If we act upon God's Word, if we take Him at His word, we will be wise, and our lives will be solidly set on the rock of

His words. If we don't take Him at His word—if we rely on our circumstances and feelings rather than what the Bible tells us, we will be foolish, building our lives upon the sand. It's really that simple. Most of us will never go through a real flood, but we will all go through the "floods of life." While we are in our personal floods, God wants us to take Him at His Word, believing that what He says is truer than how we feel or any circumstance we will ever face, because: HEAVEN AND EARTH WILL PASS AWAY, BUT HIS WORD WILL NOT PASS AWAY (Matthew 24:35).[12]

NEY BAILEY IN FAITH IS NOT A FEELING

There are rocks and bumps even on the paths of God's choosing, and we have to learn to accept them and benefit from them. The bumps are what you climb on. But this takes faith. It is much easier to kick the rock and turn around and go back. The secret to climbing higher is to look away from yourself and your difficulties, and look by faith to Jesus Christ. He knows where you are, how you feel, and what you can do. Turn it all over to Him and start walking by faith. The very rocks that seem like barriers to human eyes will, to the eyes of faith become blessings.[13]

WARREN WIERSBE IN THE BUMPS ARE WHAT YOU CLIMB ON

ENJOY HIS PRESENCE

What has God taught you today in your time alone with Him? What is your favorite promise today? Think about all you've learned about faith. Turn back to the Introduction of this study and read the Letter to the Lord that you wrote. How has God responded to the words you wrote to Him? Close by writing a new letter, a prayer of thanksgiving to your Lord for how He is teaching you to have a walk on water faith and discover power in the promises of God.

REST IN HIS LOVE

"You are a letter of Christ, cared for by us, written not with ink but with the Spirit of the living God, not on tablets of stone but on tablets of human hearts. Such confidence we have through Christ toward God. Not that we are adequate in ourselves to consider anything as coming from ourselves, but our adequacy is from God" (2 Corinthians 3:3-5).

THE VICTORY OF FAITH

This is the victory that has overcome the world—our faith. 1 John 5:4
Zion National Park, Utah, USA
Nikon D7000, ISO 160, f13.0, 3 Bracketed EXP, Adobe Photoshop, Nik Silver Efex Pro
MYPHOTOWALK.COM—CATHERINEMARTIN.SMUGMUG.COM

DEVOTIONAL READING
BY HANDLEY C.G. MOULE

DEAR FRIEND,

In your quiet times this week you have lived in Hebrews 12:1-3 and thought about the faith of Jesus and His followers. What were your most meaningful discoveries this week as you spent time with the Lord?

Most meaningful insight:

Most meaningful devotional reading:

Most meaningful verse:

Your most significant promise this week written in A Promise A Day:

Take some time to look back through the weeks of study. What are some of the most important truths you've learned about faith?

What was the most important truth you learned about faith in *Walk on Water Faith*?

What will you take with you and always remember from this study? And what was your favorite promise as you journeyed through A Promise A Day?

As you think about all that you have learned in *Walk On Water Faith*, meditate on these words by Handley C.G. Moule in *Found Faithful* about the Hebrews 11 heroes of the faith: "We have, lying around us, 'so great a cloud of witnesses' (verse 1). 'We' are running, like the competitors in the Hellenic stadium, in the public view of a mighty concourse, so vast, so aggregated, so placed aloft, that no word less great than 'cloud' occurs as its designation…True, the multitudinous watchers are unseen, but this only gives faith another opportunity of exercise; we are to treat the Blessed as seen, for we know that they are there, living to God, one with us, fellows of our life and love. So let us address ourselves afresh to the spiritual race, the course of faith… The imagery of the foot-race comes suddenly up, and in a moment raises before us the vision of the stadium and its surroundings. The reader cannot see the course with his inner eyes without also seeing those hosts of eager lookers-on which made, on every such occasion, in the old world as now, the life of the hour… But all this leaves faith in peaceful possession of a fact of unspeakable animation. It tells the discouraged or tired Christian, tempted to think of the unseen as a dark void, that it is rather a bright and populous world, in mysterious touch and continuity with this, and that our forerunners, from those of the remotest past down to the last-called beloved one who has passed out of our sight, know enough about us to mark our advance and to prepare their welcome at the goal."[14]

Therefore, since we are surrounded by such a huge crowd of witnesses to the life of faith, let us strip off every weight that slows us down, especially the sin that so easily trips us up. And let us run with endurance the race God has set before us. We do this by keeping our eyes on Jesus, the champion who initiates and perfects our faith. Because of the joy awaiting Him, He endured the cross, disregarding its shame. Now He is seated in the place of honor beside God's throne. Think of all the hostility He endured from sinful people; then you won't become weary and give up.

HEBREWS 12:1-3 NLT

Faith For The Race Set Before You

It's hard to believe that we have completed our last week of study in *Walk On Water Faith*. Today I want to look at the important words that follow Hebrews 11 and talk about how to have faith for the race set before you.

"Therefore, since we have so great a cloud of witnesses surrounding us, let us also lay aside every encumbrance and the sin which so easily entangles us, and let us run with endurance the race that is set before us, fixing our eyes on Jesus, the author and perfecter of faith..." (Hebrews 12:1-2).

What Hebrews 12:1-3 is teaching us:

1. Pay special _____ to the great cloud of witnesses surrounding us.

2. Learn the secret of an unencumbered and _____ life.

3. Understand the _____ of the race marked out before you and run with _____.

4. Keep a _____ gaze and _____ on Jesus.

5. Keep running your race _____ to the finish line.

Video messages are available on DVDs or as Digital M4V Video. Audio messages are available as Digital MP3 Audio. Visit the Quiet Time Ministries Online Store at www.quiettime.org.

NOW THAT YOU HAVE COMPLETED THESE QUIET TIMES

You have spent eight weeks consistently drawing near to God in quiet time with Him. That time alone with Him does not need to come to an end. What is the next step? To continue your pursuit of God, you might consider other books from the A Quiet Time Experience series, including *A Heart that Hopes in God, Run Before the Wind, Trusting in the Names of God,* and *Passionate Prayer.* The Quiet Times For The Heart series are also books of quiet times with titles such as *Pilgrimage of the Heart, Revive My Heart, A Heart that Dances, A Heart on Fire,* and *A Heart to See Forever.* To learn more about quiet time, read signature books from the A 30-Day Journey series such as *Six Secrets to a Powerful Quiet Time* and *Knowing and Loving the Bible.* DVD and HD Digital Leader's Kits with inspirational messages and Leader's Guides are available for many books. Quiet Time Ministries online has exciting resources like *The Quiet Time Notebooks* to encourage you in your quiet time with God. Find daily encouragement from Cath's Blog at www.quiettime. org and view A Walk In Grace, the devotional photo journal featuring Catherine's myPhotoWalk. com photography. Join hundreds of other women online to study God's Word and grow in God's grace at Ministry For Women—Google Plus Community. Resources may be ordered online from Quiet Time Ministries at www.quiettime.org or by calling Quiet Time Ministries directly. For more information, you may contact:

Quiet Time Ministries
P.O. Box 14007
Palm Desert, California 92255
(800) 925-6458, (760) 772-2357
E-mail: catherine@quiettime.org
Website: www.quiettime.org

ABOUT THE AUTHOR

Catherine Martin is a summa cum laude graduate of Bethel Theological Seminary with a Master of Arts degree in Theological Studies. She is founder and president of Quiet Time Ministries, director of women's ministries at Southwest Community Church in Indian Wells, California, and adjunct faculty member of Biola University. She is the author of *Six Secrets to a Powerful Quiet Time, Knowing and Loving the Bible, Walking with the God Who Cares, Set my Heart on Fire, Trusting in the Names of God, Passionate Prayer, Quiet Time Moments for Women,* and *Drawing Strength from the Names of God* published by Harvest House Publishers, and *Pilgrimage of the Heart, Revive My Heart* and *A Heart That Dances,* published by NavPress. She has also written *The Quiet Time Notebooks, A Heart on Fire, A Heart to See Forever, Run Before the Wind,* and *A Heart That Hopes in God,* published by Quiet Time Ministries Press. She is founder of myPhotoWalk.com dedicated to the art of devotional photography. As a popular keynote speaker at retreats and conferences, Catherine challenges others to seek God and love Him with all of their heart, soul, mind, and strength. For more information about Catherine, visit www.quiettime.org and www.myphotowalk.com.

ABOUT QUIET TIME MINISTRIES

Quiet Time Ministries is a nonprofit religious organization under Section 501(c)(3) of the Internal Revenue Code. Cash donations are tax deductible as charitable contributions. We count on prayerful donors like you, partners with Quiet Time Ministries pursuing our goals of the furtherance of the Gospel of Jesus Christ and teaching devotion to God and His Word. Visit us online at www.quiettime.org to view special funding opportunities and current ministry projects. Your prayerful donations bring countless project to life!

Quiet Time Ministries | P.O. Box 14007 | Palm Desert, California 92255
1.800.925.6458 | catherine@quiettime.org | www.quiettime.org | www.myphotowalk.com

APPENDIX

⚜ A Promise A Day ⚜

Your experience in *Walk on Water Faith* includes the discovery of power in the promises of God. God has given us His Word filled with promises to fuel our faith so that we can walk on water above and through every circumstance. What will help you to build an arsenal of promises so that when the winds begin to blow and the rain pours down you can stand strong? Ask God for *a promise a day*. Each day as you spend quiet time with the Lord in *Walk On Water Faith*, ask God to give you one promise from His Word. It may come from any part of your quiet time— Prepare Your Heart, Read and Study God's Word, Adore God in Prayer, Yield Yourself To God, Enjoy His Presence, or Rest in His Love. The promise may even come from the verse included in the special devotional photography at the end of each day's quiet time. How will you know it's the promise from the Lord for you that day? Once you have asked Him to give you a promise, then you will be open to receive the treasure of His Word for you each day. And you will notice that there will be one especially significant verse in your quiet time. It will just seem to stand out to you. Or you may not be able to get it out of your mind. Soon your spiritual eyes and ears will be tuned in and ready to see and hear God's promise for you. His promises will be more and more clear and obvious to you as you live in His Word. Some promises will be more significant than others. Asking Him for a promise a day is a journey of growth in your faith as you walk with the Lord in this quiet time experience. Once you have your promise, then write it out here in the space provided. Once you have written it, read through it again and underline any significant words or phrases. You may even want to pray it back to the Lord. Then, as God uses these promises in your life to grow your faith, you may want to mark the date and write out how God is working in your life. God bless you, dear friend, as you continue on in this great adventure of knowing Him.

WEEK ONE — STANDING STRONG WHEN THE WIND BLOW HARD

Day 1 Promise

Day 2 Promise

Day 3 Promise

Day 4 Promise

Day 5 Promise

Days 6-7 Promise

Week Two — The School of Faith

Day 1 Promise

Day 2 Promise

Day 3 Promise

Day 4 Promise

Day 5 Promise

Days 6-7 Promise

Week Three — The Gallery of Faith

Day 1 Promise

Day 2 Promise

Day 3 Promise

Day 4 Promise

Day 5 Promise

Days 6-7 Promise

WEEK FOUR — THE FAITH OF ABRAHAM

Day 1 Promise

Day 2 Promise

Day 3 Promise

Day 4 Promise

Day 5 Promise

Days 6-7 Promise

Week Five — The Faith of Moses

Day 1 Promise

Day 2 Promise

Day 3 Promise

Day 4 Promise

Day 5 Promise

Days 6-7 Promise

Week Six — The Faith of the Judges

Day 1 Promise

Day 2 Promise

Day 3 Promise

Day 4 Promise

Day 5 Promise

Days 6-7 Promise

WEEK SEVEN — THE FAITH OF THE KINGS AND THE PROPHETS

Day 1 Promise

Day 2 Promise

Day 3 Promise

Day 4 Promise

Day 5 Promise

Days 6-7 Promise

WEEK EIGHT — THE FAITH OF JESUS AND HIS FOLLOWERS

Day 1 Promise

Day 2 Promise

Day 3 Promise

Day 4 Promise

Day 5 Promise

Days 6-7 Promise

❦ DISCUSSION QUESTIONS ❦

Introduction

Begin your class with prayer and then welcome everyone to this new book of quiet times. Have the people in your group share their names and what brought them to the study. Make sure each person in your group has a book. Also, gather contact information for all participants in your group including name, address, phone number, and e-mail. That way you can keep in touch and encourage those in your group.

Familiarize your group with the layout of the book. Each week consists of five days of quiet times, as well as a devotional reading and response for days 6 and 7. Each day follows the PRAYER quiet time plan:

Prepare Your Heart

Read and Study God's Word

Adore God in Prayer

Yield Yourself to God

Enjoy His Presence

Rest in His Love

Journal and prayer pages are included in the back of the book. Also, A Promise A Day is found in the Appendix of this book. You will want to familiarize your group with asking God for a promise each day in their quiet time, then writing it on the A Promise A Day pages in the back of the book. Note that the quiet times offer devotional reading, Bible study, prayer, and practical application. Some days are longer than others and therefore, they should study at their own pace. Days 6-7 are for catching up, review, etc. This is a concentrated, intentional journey on faith. Encourage your group to interact with the study, underlining significant insights and writing comments in the margins. Encourage your group to read the Introduction sometime the first day. Also point out that the Introduction includes a place where they will write a letter to the Lord. Encourage them to draw near to God each day and ask Him to speak to their hearts.

You can determine how to organize your group sessions, but here's one idea: Discuss the week of quiet times together in the first hour, break for ten minutes, and then watch the video message on the companion DVD or HD Digital M4V. There are nine messages for *Walk On Water Faith*—one for the introduction and one for each week. You might also share with your group a summary of how to prepare for their quiet time by setting aside a time each day and a place. Consider sharing how time alone with the Lord has made a difference in your own life. Let your class know about Quiet Time Ministries Online, quiet time resources, and Catherine Martin's *A Walk In Grace Photo Journal* at www.quiettime.org.

Another option is to divide each week (completing the study in 16 weeks) by discussing days 1–3 one week and days 4–7 another week. This allows your group to journey through each quiet time at a slower pace.

Pray for one another by offering a way to record and exchange prayer requests. Some groups like to pass around a basket with cards that people can use to record prayer requests. Then, people take a request out of the basket and pray for someone during the week. Others like to use three by five cards and then exchange cards on a weekly basis.

Close this introductory class with prayer, take a short break, and then show the companion DVD or HD Digital M4V video message.

Week One: Finding Faith When The Wind Blows Hard

This week, the goal of your discussion is to begin to understand what faith is, what it looks like in action, and how you can demonstrate the kind of faith that walks on water. You will be looking at the example of Peter. This study is such an encouragement for anyone who is going through a difficult time. You will have wonderful discussions that will help your group stand strong and walk by faith in the storms of life. You want your group to be able to define faith and to realize the importance of the promises of God for their faith. They will also learn how to have faith in the fourth watch of the night: look to Jesus, listen to Jesus, respond to Jesus, believe Jesus, pray to Jesus, and worship Jesus.

This week will be a study of walk on water faith from the life of Peter. You might introduce your discussion by sharing that in this first week, your group had the opportunity to look at the walk of faith, faith when you need it most, the say-so of the Lord, when your faith is challenged, and the object of your faith. In the weeks to come, we will be looking at examples of faith in the life of Jesus and in the heroes of the faith in Hebrews 11, God's Gallery of Faith.

DAY 1: The Walk of Faith

You might begin this first week of discussion with a brief overview of what they studied. You might say something like: *This week we are looking at how we can find faith and walk on water in the storms of life.*

1. Open your discussion with prayer. Ask any new members of your group to introduce themselves. Share the goal of these quiet times: to learn about how to have a walk on water faith.

2. You began by reading the words of Paul in 2 Corinthians 5:7. Ask everyone to share how we are to live our life.

3. In your study in Day 1 you had the opportunity to read about the example of Peter in Matthew 14:22-33. Describe what happened.

4. What gave you the idea that this event was all about faith?

5. What is the definition of faith? How does this definition help you understand how to have faith?

6. What encouraged you the most in Day 1 (from the story of Fanny Crosby, the devotional reading, or the study in God's Word)?

7. How did this study today help you in beginning to think about where you are in your walk of faith?

DAY 2: Faith When You Need It Most

1. What is the fourth watch of the night and why is this sometimes the most difficult time for our faith?

2. How did Jesus encourage His disciples in the fourth watch? How was He with them in a way that they could *look to Jesus*?

3. What was significant about Jesus' words: *Take courage, it is I; do not be afraid.* Why would it have been important for them to *listen to Jesus* in their situation?

4. What did you learn about God's Word in Day 2?

5. What was your favorite promise?

6. What did you learn from the devotional reading in Yield Yourself To God?

DAY 3: The Say-So of the Lord

1. On Day 3 we looked at the say-so of the Lord. What does that mean?

2. How was Hebrews 13:5-6 a perfect example of responding to what God promises in His Word?

3. How did the words of Jesus, His say-so make a difference in the lives of the disciples, including Peter? How did they each respond?

4. What happened when Peter responded to Jesus' words?

5. What does it mean to have a walk on water faith?

6. What was your favorite quote in the devotional reading?

DAY 4: When Your Faith Is Challenged

1. In Day 4 you studied how faith is challenged. How was Fanny Crosby's faith challenged and how did she respond?

2. What are some of the ways we need to get out of the boat in order to have a walk on water faith? How can we *respond to Jesus*?

3. Describe what happened to Peter once he started walking on the water.

4. What did you learn about the importance of our focus from the example of Peter? Where should our focus be and what kind of faith does God want us to have?

5. How did Peter respond once he began to sink? How was this a demonstration of faith and what will help us to *pray to Jesus* when we find our faith wavering?

6. What promise encouraged you the most when you become afraid in a storm? How will these promises help you to *believe Jesus* when your faith is tested?

7. How did the devotional reading from Robert Parsons and D. Martyn Lloyd-Jones help you in your own faith?

8. How is your faith being challenged right now and what are you learning that encourages you in your own difficulty?

DAY 5: The Object of Your Faith

1. In Day 5 we read that biblical faith is a gift of God. And we also saw that Jesus is the object of our faith. What did the disciples learn about Jesus from this experience and how do you think it impacted their faith?

2. When the disciples *worshipped Jesus*, how did this demonstrate a transformation in their own life?

3. How did Peter grow in his relationship with Jesus?

DAYS 6 AND 7: Devotional Reading by Oswald Chambers

1. What was your favorite verse, insight, or quote from your quiet times this week?

2. What did you learn from the excerpt written by Oswald Chambers in Day 6 and 7?

3. What was your favorite promise you wrote this week in A Promise A Day?

4. What was your favorite photo this week in your quiet times?

5. What is the most important truth you learned about faith? How can you apply it in your own life? Close your time together in prayer.

Week Two: The School of Faith

The goal this week is to discover the main principles of faith from Jesus as seen in the gospels. These principles include sitting at the feet of Jesus and learning from Him, understanding great faith, learning how our faith can grow, how it is tested, and the place of surrender in our faith. You might begin by reviewing with your group what they learned last week about walk on water faith from the life of Peter. Read the short and long definitions of faith from Week One. And review how to have faith in the fourth watch of the night: look to Jesus, listen to Jesus, respond to Jesus, believe Jesus, pray to Jesus, and worship Jesus.

DAY 1: Jesus Your Teacher

1. Open your discussion with prayer. Then share that this week you had the opportunity to live in the gospels—Matthew, Mark, Luke and John— and learned about the school of faith.

2. Begin by asking "how were you encouraged by your time alone with the Lord this week?" What meant the most to you as you drew near to the Lord?

3. What did you learn about Jesus your Teacher?

4. What did Jesus teach about the Word of God in our lives?

5. What did you learn from the invitation of Jesus in Matthew 11:28-30?

6. What will help us to sit at His feet like Mary and listen to His Word?

DAY 2: When Jesus is Amazed

1. In Day 2 you studied the faith of the centurion in Luke 7:1-10. What did you learn from the centurion's faith?

2. Why was Jesus amazed and what made it a great faith?

3. Why is our decision about the authority of God's Word so important for our faith?

4. Why is it important to reason and think rightly about God's Word and how can we apply that in the midst of a difficult circumstance?

5. How is a faith walking person different than someone who isn't walking by faith?

6. What meant the most to you from the devotional reading?

DAY 3: When Your Faith Grows

1. In Day 3 you studied about how our faith can grow. What did you learn about how your faith grows from the Prepare Your Heart section of your study?

2. What did Jesus teach His disciples and show His disciples to help their faith grow?

3. What did you learn about the importance of the Holy Spirit in growing your faith? What does it mean to be filled with the Holy Spirit and how are we filled with the Holy Spirit?

4. What are some of the results of faith in our lives?

5. How is God growing your faith?

6. What did you learn from the quote by Oswald Chambers?

DAY 4: When Your Faith is Tested

1. In Day 4 you looked at the testing of your faith. What is the value of a test of faith? Share some of the verses in Prepare Your Heart that help you in understanding faith tests.

2. What did you learn from the lesson of faith in the boat on the Sea of Galilee in Matthew 8:18-28? How do we experience the same kind thing in life and what can we learn from this that will help us to have a walk on water kind of faith?

3. How was Peter's faith tested and how was Jesus involved in the care and concern of his faith?

4. What is unbelief and what is a great prayer if you are tempted with the hindrance of unbelief?

5. Are you experiencing a time of testing and what have you learned that will help you?

6. What was your favorite quote in the devotional reading?

DAY 5: The Shout of Faith

1. In Day 5 you studied the importance of surrender in walking by faith. What did you learn from the story of Mrs. Charles Cowman?

2. What did you learn from the example of Jesus that will help you in your own faith?

3. What is obedience and why is it such an integral part of faith? How did Jesus express obedience?

4. Why is abiding in Christ important for your faith?

5. How has the Lord provided for you with His very life?

6. What did you learn from the promises in Read and Study God's Word?

7. What was the most important truth you learned that is helping you to surrender

to the Lord by faith? How did the devotional reading help you? And how is He asking you to surrender?

DAYS 6 AND 7: Devotional Reading by Mrs. Charles Cowman

1. What was your favorite verse, insight, or quote from your quiet times this week?

2. What did you learn from the excerpt by Mrs. Charles Cowman in Days 6-7?

3. What was your favorite promise you wrote this week in A Promise A Day?

4. What was your favorite photo this week in your quiet times?

5. What is the most important truth you learned about walk on water faith this week? How are you in God's school of faith right now and what are you learning? Then, close in prayer.

Week Three: The Gallery of Faith

This week you are going to study and discuss Hebrews 11, God's Gallery of Faith. Hebrews 11 has also been called the Hall of Fame of Faith. You might begin your discussion by reviewing what the class discussed the last two weeks about faith including the definitions of faith. Faith is taking God at His Word. Walk on water faith is the ability to see beyond temporal circumstances to the eternal realities of God and His promises, and as a result, take God at His Word and act on His promises in spite of conflicting circumstances, thoughts, and feelings. Your goal for your discussion and study this week is to help your group see the overview of God's Gallery of Faith in Hebrews 11, understand the background of Hebrews, to discover how important our faith is to God, and how essential faith is when we become discouraged and feel like giving up.

DAY 1: What You Need When Fear Sets In

1. Open your discussion with prayer. Give a brief review of what they've learned in the last two weeks of study. Then you might begin by sharing that this week we want to look at Hebrews 11 and God's Gallery of Faith.

2. We began our quiet time experience this week by looking at the background of Hebrews 11. Why was Hebrews written?

3. One of the ways to understand the audience of Hebrews is that they were in a then and now situation. What does that mean and have you ever experienced that

yourself? Have you had a time when the trial was so difficult that even though you've known the Lord a long time, you didn't know if you would make it through?

4. Read Hebrews 13:7 and ask those in your group who has been a great example of faith for them.

5. Share your most significant insight from Day 1.

DAY 2: Finding A Faith That Pleases God

1. How did Hebrews 11:1 help you understand what faith really is?

2. According to Hebrews 11:6 what is necessary for a faith that pleases God?

3. You had an opportunity to think about faith and write your own definition of it. Would anyone like to share what they wrote?

DAY 3: Imitating The Actions of Faith

1. In Hebrews 11 we saw that faith involves action. What was the most significant action you saw as you read through the lives of those saints in Hebrews 11?

2. How did Alan Redpath's devotional reading encourage you about the life of faith?

DAY 4: The Tests of Faith

1. In Day 4 you read through Hebrews 11 and looked at how each hero of faith experienced tests of their faith. What hero's story meant the most to you in your study?

2. How did F.B. Meyer's words encourage you?

DAY 5: Discovering the Promises of Faith

1. In Day 5 you began your study looking at two ways a person can live their life. Describe those two ways from Matthew 7:24-27.

2. You read through Hebrews 11 again and looked at each hero of the faith and the promises they relied on as they walked by faith. Describe some of the promises you learned from studying different men and women in Hebrews 11.

3. How do you discover that there is great power in the promises for us to live by faith?

DAYS 6 AND 7: Devotional Reading by Annie Johnson Flint, William Lane, and D. Martyn Lloyd-Jones

1. In Days Six and Seven you had the opportunity to read from Annie Johnson Flint, William Lane, and D. Martyn Lloyd-Jones. What was your favorite truth from their writing?

2. What was your favorite verse, insight, or quote from your study in Week Three?

3. What was your favorite promise you wrote this week in A Promise A Day?

4. What was your favorite photo this week in your quiet times?

Week Four: The Faith of Abraham, The Friend of God

The goal for your discussion is to lead your group to a deeper understanding of faith by stopping in front of one of the portraits in God's Gallery of Faith. You want you group to learn more about faith from the great example of Abraham, the friend of God.

DAY 1: When You Hear God Speak

1. Open your discussion with prayer. Share briefly about your discussion last week about faith and what you learned from the overview of Hebrews 11 and God's Gallery of Faith. Review with your group the background of Hebrews and how it is a call to a new commitment for a people who are suffering and have lost confidence. In Hebrews 11 we saw that each of these heroes of the faith stepped out in faith on God's promises. And each one experienced an adversity or difficulty making the fulfillment of the promise seemingly impossible. You might begin by asking, "How have you experienced this kind of faith, where you launched out on God's promise, but found yourself challenged by a great impossibility?

2. Describe the experience of Martin Luther and how the Word of God changed his life.

3. We saw that Abraham's relationship with God began when He spoke to Abraham.

4. What did you learn about Abraham's responses to God and how were they a demonstration of faith?

5. What was your favorite part of the reading from *Men Who Met God* by A.W. Tozer?

6. How has God been speaking to your in His Word during this study?

DAY 2: When You Don't Know

1. Why was Abraham's faith such a challenge? What made his actions especially difficult?

2. What was Abraham's perspective as he traveled in life according to Hebrews 11:10 and 13-16?

3. What did you learn about Abraham's faith in Romans 4 that helps you understand faith more?

4. What do you think was the greatest encouragement to Abraham to have a hope against hope belief?

5. Have you ever experienced a time when you launched out in faith but didn't know what would happen or where you were going?

DAY 3: When You Walk With God

1. Abraham was called a friend of God. As you read the different passages of Scripture in Genesis, what did you learn from his relationship with God that encourages you to in your own walk with God?

2. What did you learn about the New Covenant and your relationship with the Lord?

3. How does an intimate relationship with the Lord help your faith? And how does faith help you in growing in your intimate relationship with the Lord?

4. What meant the most to you in the devotional reading by A.W. Tozer?

DAY 4: When You Surrender Your Dream

1. Day 4 is probably one of the most important days of study in the life of Abraham to help us understand how the promises of God impact and empower our faith. Abraham faced an impossible situation yet without denying its challenges, he grew strong in faith based on the promise instead of wavering in unbelief. You began

your study by looking at the life of Lilias Trotter. How did God's plan for her life involve surrender and what happened as a result?

2. What was God's promise to Abraham in Genesis 17:1-17?

3. How did Abraham handle that promise according to Romans 4:18-21 and what happened as a result? How can this help you in understanding how to handle God's promises and act in faith when faced with an impossible situation?

4. In Genesis 22:1-14 how was Abraham's faith tested and how did he respond?

5. What did you learn from Hebrews 11:17-19 that helps you in reasoning through God's requests and promises in your own faith?

6. Read 2 Peter 1:4. How does Abraham's example help you understand the greatness and power of God's promises?

7. Can you share a time when you were able to walk by faith in God's promise in the face of an impossible situation?

8. What is the most important truth you learned from today's study?

DAY 5: When You Receive Faith's Reward

1. How was Abraham's faith rewarded?

2. What was your most significant insight from the verses you studied in Read and Study God's Word?

3. What is righteousness and how can we have the righteousness of God. What did you learn from Galatians 3:23-29?

4. Read or sing through the words of Charles Wesley's hymn, "And Can It Be."

DAYS 6 AND 7: Devotional Reading by Lilias Trotter

1. In days 6 and 7 you had the opportunity to read from Lilias Trotter in *Parables of the Cross*. What was your favorite truth from her writing?

2. Did you have a favorite quote, insight, or verse from Week Four?

3. What was your favorite promise you wrote this week in A Promise A Day?

4. What was your favorite photo this week in your quiet times?

5. To summarize, what is the one thing you learned from Abraham that is going to help you the most in having a walk on water faith? Close your discussion together in prayer.

Week Five: The Faith of Moses, The Man of God

Your goal in your discussion this week is to help those in your group learn about faith from one of the great heroes in the Bible, Moses. Moses was a great leader who was given a great task. This week you want to learn about how to have a walk on water faith when given great tasks by the Lord, when you are faced with impossible situations, and when you need a great victory.

DAY 1: Faith That Leaves A Legacy

1. Open your discussion with prayer. Share briefly about your discussion Abraham and how he is such an example of faith for us. Then talk about how we are learning about faith and how we can have a walk on water faith, experiencing victory in the midst of impossible circumstances. Now, this week, we have spent time in God's Gallery of Faith in front of the portrait of Moses, the Man of God. We are going to learn powerful lessons of faith from this hero of the faith who is one of our great examples. As you begin your time of discussion today, read the quote by F.B. Meyer on the Week Five page.

2. Describe the circumstances surrounding Moses' birth.

3. How was his mother, Jochebed such a hero of the faith? How does she inspire your own faith and how your life can leave a legacy to those around you?

DAY 2: Faith When Your Heart Is Faint

1. Now we are going to talk about Moses. And we saw that he surely was not perfect. What does Alan Redpath mean by the statement, "The Bible never flatters its heroes"?

2. God met Moses on Mt. Horeb. Describe how God spoke to Moses. What was He asking of Moses and how did Moses respond?

3. Why do you think Moses was trying to run from the task God has for him?

4. How do you think Moses became so humble and how does humility help us have great faith?

5. What do you learn from Moses for the times when your own heart feels faint?

DAY 3: Faith For The Impossible

1. Once Moses arrived in Egypt to carry out God's task for him, what were the impossibles that faced him?

2. How did God deal with the impossible situation as His people stood at the Red Sea with the Egyptians chasing them?

3. What was your favorite insight from the devotional reading in Day 3?

4. How has God encouraged you for victory in your own impossible circumstances? Ask if anyone would like to share a time when the Lord took them through a Red Sea experience and helped them overcome in the midst of it by faith.

DAY 4: Faith For Intimacy With God

1. Moses experienced an intimate relationship with God and you can too. That's our goal as we talk about our study in Day 4. We want learn from Moses so we can know an intimate relationship with the Lord.

2. How did the devotional reading by Andrew Murray in Prepare Your Heart help you understand Moses? Describe what you learned about Moses and loved best from that reading.

3. What did you learn about the relationship between God and Moses in Exodus 33:9-23?

4. What did Moses ask of God and how did God respond? What did Moses learn about God according to the verses you studied in Exodus 34?

5. How do you think Moses' experience with God grew his faith in God?

6. What was your favorite insight from the devotional reading in Day 4?

DAY 5: Faith To Pass It On

1. In Day 5 we saw Moses nearing the end of his life. Have someone read Deuteronomy 3:2-6. Why was Moses not able to go into the Promised Land?

2. What two heroes of the faith are listed in Hebrews 11:30-31 and what happened because of faith?

3. What did you learn about Moses and Joshua? How do you think Joshua learned so much about the Lord and became such a great leader?

4. What is the most important truth you learned in Day 5?

DAYS 6 AND 7: Devotional Reading by Andrew Murray

1. What was your favorite verse, insight, or quote from your quiet times this week?

2. What did you learn from the excerpt by Andrew Murray?

3. What was your favorite promise you wrote this week in A Promise A Day?

4. What was your favorite photo this week in your quiet times?

5. Close your time together in prayer.

Week Six: The Faith of the Judges

In Week Six you are continuing your walk through God's Gallery of Faith and are stopping in front of the portraits given to us in verse 32 of names that many in your group may not have heard of before their week of study. These are the names of Judges and because they are in God's Gallery of Faith, we want to see what the Lord wants to teach us from their lives. The goal for your discussion is to help your group understand the life and times of these judges and how they can have faith in God's promises even in the most difficult seasons of life.

DAY 1: When You Need To Lead

1. Open your discussion with prayer. Share briefly about your discussion last week about Moses and his faith. Now, this week, we have spent time in Judges looking at various portraits found in one small verse in Hebrews 11:32. You might ask someone to read Hebrews 11:32 as you begin your discussion. Also have someone read John MacArthur's quote on the beginning section page of Week Six.

2. We began with the life of J. Gresham Machen. Share what you learned from his life, how his life encouraged you, and the importance of 2 Chronicles 16:9. You might have someone in your group read this powerful verse.

3. Ask those in your group to describe the times of the Judges.

4. Who was Deborah? Describe her leadership and how she demonstrated faith in God.

5. How did Deborah rely on the Lord according to Judges 5:1-4?

6. What promises meant the most to you when you need help and guidance?

7. How has God met you with personally in a time when you desperately needed His help and guidance?

DAY 2: When You Are In A Battle

1. Have someone read Prepare Your Heart in Day 2 as you begin your study. Then ask what means the most to them in that reading today?

2. What did you learn about Barak and why do you think he is in God's Gallery of Faith?

3. How are we in a battle today and what did you learn from Paul and Peter that will help you in your spiritual battle? What promises can you count on by faith when the enemy comes against you?

DAY 3: When You Feel Forgotten

1. Now we look at Gideon and how to have faith when you feel forgotten. In what way did Gideon feel forgotten?

2. How did God come to Gideon and how do you think His words were a promise to give power to Gideon and grow his faith in the Lord?

3. What was the most important truth you learned from the life of Gideon and why do you think his name is included in God's Gallery of faith?

4. What promise encouraged and empowered you in today's study?

5. How did the devotional reading encourage you?

DAY 4: When Everything Is Against You

1. Now we are going to stop in front of the portrait of another hero of the faith—Jephthah. How was everything against Jephthah?

2. Describe how he became a leader, his relationship with the Lord, and the turn of events in his life.

3. How did God provide for Jephthah?

4. How are you encouraged, challenged, and cautioned by the faith and the life of Jephthah?

DAY 5: When You Need Grace

1. How did God use Samson in his day and time?

2. What did you learn from the life of Samson?

3. What truths did you learn from the devotional reading and the verses in today's quiet time that encourage you when you need grace?

DAYS 6 AND 7: Devotional Reading by Mrs. Charles Cowman

1. What was your favorite verse, insight, or quote from your quiet times this week?

2. What did you learn from the excerpt by Mrs. Charles Cowman?

3. What was your favorite promise you wrote this week in A Promise A Day?

4. What was your favorite photo this week in your quiet times?

5. Close in prayer.

Week Seven: The Faith of the Kings and the Prophets

The goal for your discussion this week is to learn and grow in faith as a result of the examples of those mentioned in Hebrews 11:32—David, Samuel and the Prophets.

DAY 1: When You Are God's Servant

1. Open your discussion with prayer. Share briefly about all that we have been studying about faith. Begin by having your group define faith. Review what it means to have a walk on water faith. Talk about the background of Hebrews and the importance of God's Gallery of Faith to encourage us to run our race with endurance when the winds are blowing hard in our life. Once you have reviewed what we have studied thus far, ask your group how they are being encouraged in their faith with this study.

2. Now, this week, we looked at the life of David, Samuel and the prophets. Begin by having someone read the quote by Charles Haddon Spurgeon on the Week 7 main section page.

3. What did it mean to be a prophet of God?

4. How did God choose Samuel and how do you think God helped him grow in his faith?

5. What did you see about Samuel that showed he was a man of faith?

6. How do you think Samuel's faith was tested?

7. How do you think Samuel overcame his disappointments and continued to walk by faith?

8. What did you learn from Samuel that helps you in your own faith and in your ministry?

9. What was your favorite part of the devotional reading?

DAY 2: When You Love God

1. In Day 2 we looked at the life of David. How did God grow David's faith and what do you think helped David become a man after God's own heart?

2. How was David's faith tested?

3. What was your favorite promise from Psalm 37 that encouraged you in your own faith?

4. What was significant to you in the devotional reading?

DAY 3: When You Are Called By God

1. In Day 3 you looked at the life and faith of Isaiah, one of God's great prophets. How did God issue His call to Isaiah and how do you think the call encouraged and challenged Isaiah's faith?

2. How was Isaiah's faith challenged in ministry?

3. What was your favorite promise in Isaiah?

DAY 4: When You Are Broken

1. In Day 4, you studied the life and faith of Jeremiah. What were the great promises God gave to Jeremiah when He called him into service as a prophet? How do you think these promises empowered and encouraged Jeremiah during his ministry?

2. How was Jeremiah's faith tested?

3. What did you learn from Jeremiah in Lamentations 3 that encouraged your own faith?

4. What meant the most to you in Day 4?

DAY 5: When You Question God

1. When did Habakkuk's prophecy occur in the history of God's people?

2. What were Habakkuk's questions and how was his faith being tested?

3. How can you tell Habakkuk's faith was growing?

4. What encouraged you from the life and words of Habakkuk?

5. What was your favorite insight from Day 5?

DAYS 6 AND 7: Devotional Reading by Norman Grubb

1. What was your favorite verse, insight, or quote from your quiet times this week?

2. What was your favorite insight from the words of Norman Grubb?

3. How is God growing you in your ability to have a walk on water faith?

4. What was your favorite promise you wrote this week in A Promise A Day?

5. What was your favorite photo this week in your quiet times?

6. Close your time together in prayer.

Week Eight: The Faith of Jesus and His Followers

The goal of your discussion is to help your group share what they've learned from Hebrews 12:1-3, the example of Jesus, and the Lord's disciples in the 1st Century Early Church. Help them realize that now is their time and their opportunity of faith in running the race set before them. You will want to allow time for sharing all that those in your group have learned in *Walk On Water Faith*.

DAY 1: For the Joy Set Before Him—Jesus

1. Open your discussion with prayer. Begin by expressing how much you've enjoyed leading the group and sharing together during this journey of faith. And share how wonderful the discussions have been. As you discuss together for one last time in *Walk on Water Faith*, ask your group what has been their favorite part of this study.

2. This week we looked at Hebrews 12:1-3, the words that follow the great Hebrews 11 chapter. And we studied Jesus, His followers, and what it means for us to run our own race in life. Begin by having someone read Hebrews 12:1-3. Ask your group to share what the Lord is asking us to do in these verses?

3. What did you learn from Peter in 1 Peter 1:7-9 about faith and the proof of your faith?

4. What did you learn from Jesus about how to suffer by faith? Share about the "joy set before Him."

5. What are some of the joys we are given because of Christ?

6. What was your favorite quote from your quiet time in Day 1?

DAY 2: Run The Race Set Before You

1. What did you learn from the verses you read that will help you run with endurance the race set before you?

2. What two hindrances are we to lay aside? What are the kinds of things that can become encumbrances in our lives and keep us from running our race?

3. How are we to handle sin and why does sin keep us from running our race?

4. How has God been working in your own life to encourage you and help you run your own race? How has He been growing your faith and endurance?

5. What encouraged you the most in Day 2?

DAY 3: The Women of Faith

1. How does the life of Vonette Bright encourage you?

2. Who were some of the women of faith during the time of Jesus and in the Early Church, and how did their faith encourage you?

3. What encouraged you the most in your faith in Day 3?

DAY 4: Fight the Fight of Faith—Paul

1. Begin by having someone read the words of Acts 20:24 and ask how those words encourage your faith today.

2. What did you learn from the verses from Paul that help you to fight the fight of faith?

3. Share what Oswald Chambers wrote about faith and what his words mean to you?

4. Read together 2 Timothy 4:7-8 and ask what they loved the most about those words?

5. What was your favorite quote from Day 4?

DAY 5: Your Life Speaks, So Fix Your Eyes On Jesus

1. On Day 5 you studied that there is a message spoken by your life and that your life speaks. What does that mean? And how does that challenge you today?

2. What kind of life and relationship does Jesus invite you to in Mark 6:31 and John 15:1-11? What are the greatest challenges to this kind of life and relationship with the Lord? How might these be considered a test of your faith?

3. What did you learn from the verses you read about the message of your life?

4. What was your favorite quote from your Day 5 quiet time?

5. How did God answer the prayer that you wrote in your letter to Him at the beginning of the study? Would you like to share anything from the prayer of thanksgiving that you wrote as you closed your Day 5 quiet time?

DAYS 6 AND 7: Devotional Reading by Handley C.G. Moule

1. What encouraged you from the excerpt from Handley C.G. Moule

2. What was your favorite promise you wrote this week in A Promise A Day?

3. You had an opportunity to take some time and leaf through these eights weeks of quiet times to look at all you have learned. What are some of the most important principles and truths we've learned about faith in this study?

4. What is the most important truth you have learned about faith in this book of quiet times? What will you take with you? (If you have a visual aid such as a whiteboard, you might even write these truths out for your class to see).

5. What was your favorite promise written in A Promise A Day for the entire study?

6. What was your favorite photo in *Walk on Water Faith*? In what way was the devotional photography meaningful to you in your quiet times?

7. If you didn't answer before, would you like to share how God answered the prayer that you wrote in your letter to Him at the beginning of the study?

8. What will you take with you from *Walk On Water Faith*? What will you always remember?

9. Close in prayer.

NOTES

WEEK 1

1. Ney Bailey, *Faith is Not a Feeling* (Colorado Springs: Waterbrook Press, 2002), p. 31.

2. Prayer taken from *The Valley of Vision* published by The Banner of Truth Trust, copyright Arthur Bennet 1975, used here by permission. www.banneroftruth.org.

3. Octavius Winslow, *Help Heavenward* (Carlisle: The Banner of Truth Trust, 2000), p. 1.

4. Fanny Crosby, *Fanny J. Crosby, An Autobiography* (Peabody: Hendrickson Publishers, 2008) p. 96.

5. Catherine Martin, *A Heart To See Forever - Embrace The Promise Of The Eternal Perspective* (Palm Desert: Quiet Time Ministries, 2003) p. 14

6. Corrie ten Boom, *Each New Day,* (Grand Rapids: Fleming H. Revell, 1977) p. 18.

7. Miles J. Stanford, *Principles of Spiritual Growth* (Lincoln: Back to the Bible, 1987) p. 6.

8. F.B. Meyer, *Daily Prayers* (Wheaton: Harold Shaw Publishers, 1995) p. 18.

9. Taken from *My Utmost For His Highest* by Oswald Chambers, © 1935 by Dodd Mead & Co., renewed © 1963 by the Oswald Chambers Publications Assn. Ltd. Used by permission of Discovery House Publishers, Box 3566, Grand Rapids, MI 49501. All rights reserved, p. 156-157, June 4-5 selection.

10. Catherine Marshall ed., *The Prayers of Peter Marshall,* (Grand Rapids: Chosen Books, 1982), p. 18.

11. Robert Parsons, *Quotes from the Quiet Hour,* (Chicago: Moody Press, 1949) pp. 27-28.

12. D. Martyn Lloyd-Jones, *Studies in Sermon on the Mount* (Grand Rapids: Wm. Be. Eerdmans Publishing Company 1971, 1979) pp. 129-134.

13. Corrie ten Boom, *Each New Day,* p. 42.

14. Taken from *My Utmost For His Highest* by Oswald Chambers, © 1935 by Dodd Mead & Co., renewed © 1963 by the Oswald Chambers Publications Assn. Ltd. Used by permission of Discovery House Publishers, Box 3566, Grand Rapids, MI 49501. All rights reserved, p. 304, October 30 selection.

WEEK 2

1. Warren Wiersbe, *Be Skillful* (Wheaton: Victor Books, 1996).

2. Mrs. Charles Cowman, *Springs in the Valley* (The Oriental Missionary Society, 1944), p. 368.

3. Robert Parsons, *Quotes from the Quiet Hour,* (Chicago: Moody Press, 1949) p. 77.

4. Andrew Murray, *The Inner Life* (New York: Fleming H. Revell 1905) pp. 97-100.

5. F.B. Meyer, *Daily Prayers* (Wheaton: Harold Shaw Publishers, 1995) p. 74.

6. Taken from *My Utmost For His Highest* by Oswald Chambers, © 1935 by Dodd Mead & Co., renewed © 1963 by the Oswald Chambers Publications Assn. Ltd. Used by permission of Discovery House Publishers, Box 3566, Grand Rapids, MI 49501. All rights reserved, p. 305, October 31 selection.

7. Mrs. Charles Cowman, *Streams in the Desert,* June 2.

8. Miles J. Stanford, *Complete Words of Miles J. Stanford* (Galaxie Software 2001).

9. Excerpted from *Can You Drink The Cup?* by Henri J.M. Nouwen. Copyright © 1996, 2006 by Ave Maria Press®, Inc., P.O. Box 428, Notre Dame, IN 46556, www.avemariapress.com. Used with permission of the publisher, pp. 40-41.

10. Taken from *My Utmost For His Highest* by Oswald Chambers, © 1935 by Dodd Mead & Co., renewed © 1963 by the Oswald Chambers Publications Assn. Ltd. Used by permission of Discovery House Publishers, Box 3566, Grand Rapids, MI 49501. All rights reserved, p. 305, October 31 selection.

WEEK 3

1. Charles Haddon Spurgeon, *Morning and Evening*, May 2 Evening Selection.

2. William Lane, *Hebrews, A Call To Commitment* (Peabody: Hendrickson Publishers, 1985), p. 148.

3. Corrie ten Boom, *This Day is the Lord's* (Old Tappan: Fleming H. Revell, 1979) p. 82.

4. William Lane, *Hebrews, A Call To Commitment*, p. 26.

5. William Lane, *Hebrews, A Call To Commitment*, p. 149.

6. Kenneth Wuest, Wuest's Word Studies (Grand Rapids: Eerdmans, 1997) Hebrews 11:1 selection.

7. F.B. Meyer, *Daily Prayers* (Wheaton: Harold Shaw Publishers, 1995) p. 31.

8. F.B. Meyer, *The Devotional Commentary*, (Wheaton: Tyndale House Publishers, 1989) p. 603.

9. Alan Redpath, *Faith For The Times* (Grand Rapids: Baker Book House, 1976) p. 42.

10. F.B. Meyer, *Tried By Fire*, (Fort Washington: Christian Literature Crusade 1977) p. 34.

11. James McNeill, *The Sunken City*, (New York: Scholastic Book Services 1964) p. 11.

12. Ruth Harms Calkin, *Lord, I Keep Running Back To You* (Wheaton: Tyndale House Publishers 1987) p. 22.

13. Nick Harrison, Power in the Promises (Grand Rapids: Zondervan Publishing House, 2013) p. 36.

14. Annie Johnson Flint, *Best-Loved Poems*, (Toronto: Evangelical Publishers) p. 105.

15. William Lane, *Hebrews, A Call To Commitment*, p. 156.

16. D. Martyn Lloyd-Jones, *Studies in Sermon on the Mount* (Grand Rapids: Wm. Be. Eerdmans Publishing Company 1971, 1979) pp. 115-116.

WEEK 4

1. F.B. Meyer, *Great Men of the Bible, Volume 1* (Grand Rapids: Zondervan Publishing House, 1981) p. 32.

2. F.B. Meyer, *Daily Prayers* (Wheaton: Harold Shaw Publishers, 1995) p. 10.

3. A.W. Tozer, *Men Who Met God* (Camp Hill: Christian Publications 1986) pp. 19-22.

4. Barclay M. Newman and Eugene A. Nida, *A Translator's Handbook on Paul's Letter to the Romans* (New York: United Bible Societies 1973) pp. 86-87.

5. Brian Croft, *A Faith That Endures,* (Leominster: Day One Publications 2011) pp. 38-39.

6. Dwight Hervey Small, *No Rival Love*, (Fort Washington: Christian Literature Crusade 1983) p.88.

7. Lyle Dorsett, *A Passion For God* (Chicago: Moody Publishers 2008) p. 122.

8. A.W. Tozer, *The Pursuit of God* (Camp Hill: Christian Publications, 1993)

9. A.W. Tozer, *Men Who Met God*, pp. 13-14.

10. Miriam Huffman Rockness, *A Passion for the Impossible* (Grand Rapids: Discovery House Publishers 2003) p. 83.

11. Richard Rushing ed., Voices From The Past (Carlisle: The Banner of Truth Trust 2009, 2010) p. 193.

12. F.B. Meyer, *Great Men of the Bible Volume 1*, p. 56.

13. Lilias Trotter, *Parables of the Cross*, (London: Marshall Brothers n.d.) p. 21.

WEEK 5

1. F.B. Meyer, *Great Men of the Bible, Volume 1* (Grand Rapids: Zondervan Publishing House, 1981) p. 153.

2. Noel Piper, *Faithful Women and Their Extraordinary God* (Wheaton: Crossway Books 2005), p. 22.

3. F.B. Meyer, *Great Men of the Bible, Volume 1, p. 156.*

4. John S.B. Monsell, L.L.D., *Parish Musings* (London: Gilbert and Rivington 1864) p. 9.

5. A.W. Tozer, *Men Who Met God* (Camp Hill: Christian Publications 1986) p. 84.

6. Annie Johnson Flint, *Best-Loved Poems*, (Toronto: Evangelical Publishers) p. 23.

7. Andrew Murray, *The Inner Life* ((New York: Fleming H. Revell 1905) p. 32.

8. F.B. Meyer, *Great Men of the Bible, Volume 1,* p. 153.

9. F.B. Meyer, *Daily Prayers* (Wheaton: Harold Shaw Publishers, 1995) p. 79.

10. Charles Haddon Spurgeon, *Morning and Evening*, June 30 Evening Selection..

11. Andrew Murray, *The Inner Life*, pp. 11-13.

WEEK 6

1. John MacArthur, *Anxious for Nothing* (Colorado Springs: David C. Cook 1993, 2012), p. 45.

2. Ned B. Stonehouse, *J. Gresham Machen* (Grand Rapids: Wm. B. Eerdmans Publishing Company 1954) Preface.

3. Personal Note: *New Testament Greek For Beginners* by Machen was my textbook at Bethel Theological Seminary.

4. Ned B. Stonehouse, *J. Gresham Machen*, p. 394.

5. Frank E. Gaebelein, Earl S. Kalland, Donald H. Madvig, Herbert Wold, F.B. Huey Jr. and Ronald F. Youngblood, *The Expositor's Bible Commentary: Deuteronomy, Joshua, Judges, Ruth, 1 & 2 Samuel, Vol. 3* (Grand Rapids: Zondervan Publishing House 1992).

6. F.B. Meyer, *Daily Prayers* (Wheaton: Harold Shaw Publishers, 1995) p. 58.

7. J. Gresham Machen, *What Is Faith?* (Grand Rapids: Wm. B. Eerdmans Publishing Company 1946), pp. 118-119.

8. Warren Wiersbe, *What To Wear To The War* (Lincoln: Back To The Bible, 19986) pp. 5-6.

9. Taken from *My Utmost For His Highest* by Oswald Chambers, © 1935 by Dodd Mead & Co., renewed © 1963 by the Oswald Chambers Publications Assn. Ltd. Used by permission of Discovery House Publishers, Box 3566, Grand Rapids, MI 49501. All rights reserved, p. 304, October 30 selection.

10. Warren Wiersbe, *What To Wear To The War*, pp. 11-12.

11. Pastor and Author Jim Smoke went home to be with the Lord on May 20, 2014. He was my dear friend. And I was the one who visited him that one last time.

12. Mrs. Charles Cowman, *Streams in the Desert* (The Oriental Missionary Society) p. 212.

13. Robert J. Morgan, *Then Sings My Soul*, (Nashville: Thomas Nelson Publishers 2003) p. 179.

14. Frank E. Gaebelein, Earl S. Kalland, Donald H. Madvig, Herbert Wold, F.B. Huey Jr. and Ronald F. Youngblood, *The Expositor's Bible Commentary: Deuteronomy, Joshua, Judges, Ruth, 1 & 2 Samuel, Vol. 3* (Grand Rapids: Zondervan Publishing House 1992).

15. Charles Haddon Spurgeon, *Beside Still Waters*.

16. Robert Parsons, *Quotes from the Quiet Hour*, (Chicago: Moody Press, 1949) p. 56.

17. Amy Carmichael, *Mountain Breezes: The Collected Poems of Amy Carmichael* © 1999 by the Dohnavur Fellowship. Used by permission of CLC Publications. May not be further reproduced. All rights reserved.

18. Mrs. Charles Cowman, *Streams in the Desert*, p. 336.

19. Mrs. Charles Cowman, *Streams in the Desert*, p. 330.

WEEK 7

1. Charles Haddon Spurgeon, *Morning and Evening*, June 20 Morning Selection.

2. Geoffrey W. Bromiley, ed, *The International Standard Bible Encyclopedia*, Revised (Grand Rapids: Wm. Be Eerdmans, 1979-1988)

3. Charles Haddon Spurgeon, *Beside Still Waters*, January 27 selection.

4. F.B. Meyer, *Daily Prayers* (Wheaton: Harold Shaw Publishers, 1995) p. 130.

5. Alan Redpath, *The Making Of A Man Of God* (Old Tappan: Fleming H. Revell 1962) p. 67.

6. Ronald F. Youngblood, *The Book of Isaiah*, (Grand Rapids: Baker Books 1984) p. 10.

7. Ruth Harms Calkin, *Lord, I Keep Running Back To You* (Wheaton: Tyndale House Publishers 1987), p. 85.

8. F.B. Meyer, *Great Men of the Bible, Volume 2* (Grand Rapids: Zondervan Publishing House, 1982) pp. 151-153.

9. From the Northumbria Community, *Celtic Daily Prayer*, (San Francisco: HarperCollins 1994) p.65.

10. John MacArthur, Anxious For Nothing (Colorado Springs: David C. Cook 1993, 2012) pp. 74-75.

11. Norman Grubb, *Touching the Invisible*, (Toronto: The Studd Press n.d.) p. 32.

WEEK 8

1. W.H. Griffith Thomas, *The Christian Life and How To Live It*, (Chicago: Moody Press, 1913) p. 126.

2. Meyer, *Daily Prayers* (Wheaton: Harold Shaw Publishers, 1995) p. 92.

3. Warren Wiersbe, *The Bumps are What You Climb On* (Grand Rapids: Baker Book House 1980, 2002) pp. 14-15.

4. Fritz Rienecker and Cleon Rogers, *Linguistic Key to the Greek New Testament*, (Grand Rapids: Zondervan Publishing House 1976) p. 705.

5. William Lane, *Hebrews, A Call To Commitment*, (Peabody: Hendrickson Publishers 1985) p. 159.

6. Helen Kooiman Hosier, *100 Christian Women who Changed the 20th Century* (Grand Rapids: Fleming H. Revell, 2000) p. 300.

7. Vonette Bright, *In His Hands: Finding A Faith That Will Sustain You, Encourage You, and Give You Hope* (Ventura: Gospel Light 2010) Preface.

8. Taken from *My Utmost For His Highest* by Oswald Chambers, © 1935 by Dodd Mead & Co., renewed © 1963 by the Oswald Chambers Publications Assn. Ltd. Used by permission of Discovery House Publishers, Box 3566, Grand Rapids, MI 49501. All rights reserved, p. 304, October 30 selection..

9. Mrs. Charles Cowman, *Streams in the Desert*, (The Oriental Missionary Society) p. 185.

10. Professor James Stewart, *The Strong Name*, (Edinburgh: T. and T. Clark 1940) p. 78

11. John S.B. Monsell, L.L.D., *Parish Musings* (London: Gilbert and Rivington 1864) pp. 39-40.

12. Ney Bailey, *Faith Is Not A Feeling* (Colorado Springs: Waterbrook Press 2002) pp. 32, 112, 135.

13. Warren Wiersbe, *The Bumps are What You Climb On*, p. 14.

14. Elizabeth Skoglund, *Found Faithful*, (Grand Rapids: Discovery House Publishers 2003) pp. 307-309.

❧ ACKNOWLEDGMENTS ❧

How does a book like *Walk On Water Faith* come about? It takes years of God etching these principles from the Word of God on the heart in such a way that it is lived out in life. I have had this book of quiet times in my heart for a long time. However, God needed to take me on a few difficult roads and a long journey before it was time for *Walk On Water Faith*. This is the fifth in the A Quiet Time Experience series—quiet times for the busy person to use in their quiet time to go deep with God and grow in their intimate relationship with Him.

Thank you to my precious family; David, Mother, Dad (now home with the Lord), Rob, Kayla, Christopher, Andy, Keegan, and James. Thank you especially for your unconditional love and encouragement as I write books and share the message that God has laid on my heart in my quiet times alone with Him.

I want to especially thank my husband, David, for your love, wisdom, and brilliance as together we run this race set before us. And thank you for the beautiful cover design of *Walk On Water Faith*.

I am so very thankful over these many years for the Quiet Time Ministries team for serving the Lord together with me—Kayla Branscum, Shirley Peters (now home with the Lord), Conni Hudson, Cindy Clark, Sandy Fallon, Karen Darras, and Kelly Abeyratne.

And then, thank you for dear friends who have offered such words of truth, encouragement, and hope that I have needed all along the way: Beverly Trupp, Andy Kotner Graybill, Julie Airis, Cindy Clark, and Vonette Bright.

Thank you to Johnny Mann (now home with the Lord) for writing the beautiful music of "Quiet Time" and for his wife, Betty Mann. Your encouragement over the years has meant so much to me.

Thank you Stefanie Kelly, for your amazing music, especially "I Know He Knows."

A special thank you to Ney Bailey for your words of wisdom over the years and especially for teaching me about faith early on when I heard you speak and also in *Faith Is Not A Feeling*.

Thank you to the Board of Directors of Quiet Time Ministries: David Martin, Conni Hudson, Andy Kotner Graybill, and Jane Lyons, for your faithfulness in this ministry. And thank you to all who have partnered with me both financially and prayerfully in Quiet Time Ministries. You have helped make possible this idea the Lord gave me so many years ago called Quiet Time Ministries. Thank you to the Enriching Your Quiet Time magazine staff for helping develop these ideas on faith: Conni Hudson, Maurine Cromwell, Julie Airis, and Cay Hough.

Thank you to the staff at Southwest Church for loving the Lord. Thank you to the women at Southwest Church—it is such a joy and privilege to serve the Lord together with you.

Thank you to those who have been such a huge help to me in the writing and publishing of books: Jim Smoke (now home with the Lord) whose advice and help have, by God's grace, completely altered the course of my life and Greg Johnson, my agent, who has come alongside me and Quiet Time Ministries to help in the goals that the Lord has laid on my heart.

I am especially grateful and thankful for Bill Fortney who has encouraged me so much in my devotional photography and taught me through His Light Workshops on the amazing journeys through Monument Valley, Bryce, Zion National Park, and Antelope Canyon. Thank you, Bill, and the entire team, for taking us to so many amazing places to capture beautiful images of God's amazing majesty including the ones from Zion contained in this book (and online in color at CatherineMartin.SmugMug.com). And then, I am so grateful to Scott Kelby for his instruction at KelbyOne.com to learn photography, Lightroom, and Photoshop. A special thanks to Trey Ratcliff for teaching me all about HDR and inspiring me to be creative and think outside of the box when it comes to photography. Thank you to Steve Cirone for teaching me all about bird photography. And finally, thank you to Laurie Rubin, my wildlife photography mentor, who has helped me grow and learn in how I see and compose images.

A special thanks to all those leaders who answer God's call to lead others and challenge them to draw near to God, study His Word, and live for His glory. And a special thanks to all the groups worldwide who are drawing near to God in quiet time using the different quiet time studies from Quiet Time Ministries.

Finally, thank you to all those saints who have the run the race before and shown me that I could take God at His Word and walk on water with my faith; especially Corrie ten Boom, Charles Haddon Spurgeon, Oswald Chambers, Octavius Winslow, Amy Carmichael, and Annie Johnson Flint.

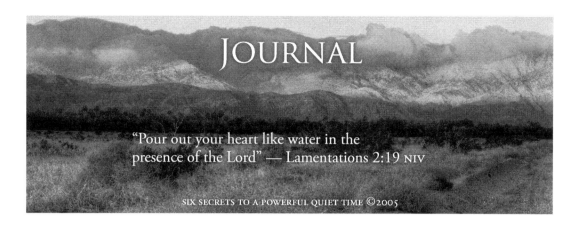

JOURNAL

"Pour out your heart like water in the
presence of the Lord" — Lamentations 2:19 NIV

SIX SECRETS TO A POWERFUL QUIET TIME ©2005

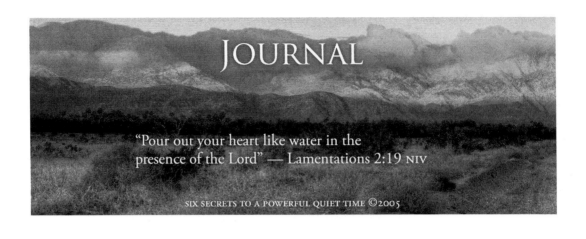

JOURNAL

"Pour out your heart like water in the presence of the Lord" — Lamentations 2:19 NIV

SIX SECRETS TO A POWERFUL QUIET TIME ©2005

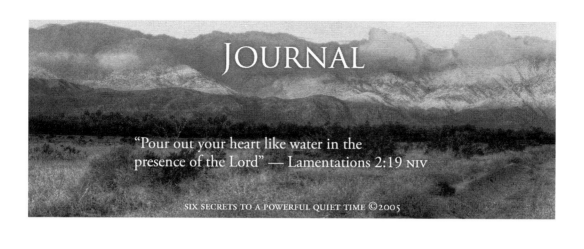

JOURNAL

"Pour out your heart like water in the presence of the Lord" — Lamentations 2:19 NIV

JOURNAL

"Pour out your heart like water in the presence of the Lord" — Lamentations 2:19 NIV

SIX SECRETS TO A POWERFUL QUIET TIME ©2005

....

....

....

....

....

....

....

....

....

....

....

....

....

....

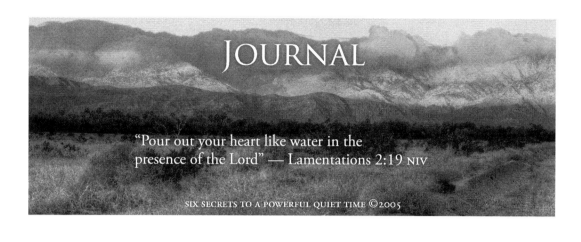

JOURNAL

"Pour out your heart like water in the
presence of the Lord" — Lamentations 2:19 NIV

SIX SECRETS TO A POWERFUL QUIET TIME ©2005

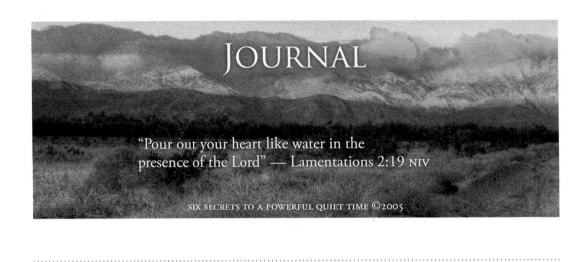

JOURNAL

"Pour out your heart like water in the presence of the Lord" — Lamentations 2:19 NIV

SIX SECRETS TO A POWERFUL QUIET TIME ©2005

ADORE GOD IN PRAYER

"Don't worry about anything; instead, pray about everything" — Philippians 4:6 NIV

*Prayer for*_____

Date: Topic:

Scripture:

Request:

Answer:

Date: Topic:

Scripture:

Request:

Answer:

Date: Topic:

Scripture:

Request:

Answer:

Date: Topic:

Scripture:

Request:

Answer:

Date: Topic:

Scripture:

Request:

Answer:

ADORE GOD IN PRAYER

"Don't worry about anything;
instead, pray about everything" — Philippians 4:6 NIV

SIX SECRETS TO A POWERFUL QUIET TIME ©2005

*Prayer for*_____

Date: Topic:

Scripture:

Request:

Answer:

Date: Topic:

Scripture:

Request:

Answer:

Date: Topic:

Scripture:

Request:

Answer:

Date: Topic:

Scripture:

Request:

Answer:

Date: Topic:

Scripture:

Request:

Answer:

ADORE GOD IN PRAYER

"Don't worry about anything;
instead, pray about everything" — Philippians 4:6 NIV

SIX SECRETS TO A POWERFUL QUIET TIME ©2005

*Prayer for*_____

Date: Topic:

Scripture:

Request:

Answer:

Date: Topic:

Scripture:

Request:

Answer:

Date: Topic:

Scripture:

Request:

Answer:

Date: Topic:

Scripture:

Request:

Answer:

Date: Topic:

Scripture:

Request:

Answer:

ADORE GOD IN PRAYER

"Don't worry about anything;
instead, pray about everything" — Philippians 4:6 NIV

SIX SECRETS TO A POWERFUL QUIET TIME ©2005

*Prayer for*_____

Date: Topic:
Scripture:
Request:

Answer:

_____

Date: Topic:
Scripture:
Request:

Answer:

_____

Date: Topic:
Scripture:
Request:

Answer:

_____

Date: Topic:
Scripture:
Request:

Answer:

_____

Date: Topic:
Scripture:
Request:

Answer:

_____

ADORE GOD IN PRAYER

"Don't worry about anything; instead, pray about everything" — Philippians 4:6 NIV

*Prayer for*_____

Date: Topic:
Scripture:
Request:

Answer:

___

Date: Topic:
Scripture:
Request:

Answer:

___

Date: Topic:
Scripture:
Request:

Answer:

___

Date: Topic:
Scripture:
Request:

Answer:

___

Date: Topic:
Scripture:
Request:

Answer:

___

*Prayer for*_____

Date: Topic:
Scripture:
Request:

Answer:

Date: Topic:
Scripture:
Request:

Answer:

Date: Topic:
Scripture:
Request:

Answer:

Date: Topic:
Scripture:
Request:

Answer:

Date: Topic:
Scripture:
Request:

Answer:

CATHERINE MARTIN

Author of *Six Secrets To A Powerful Quiet Time*

THE QUIET TIME NOTEBOOK

The PRAYER Quiet Time Plan

CATHERINE MARTIN
Author of *The Quiet Time Notebook*

THE
QUIET TIME
JOURNAL

Pouring Out Your Soul To The Lord

Made in the USA
Lexington, KY
16 January 2017